A JOURNEY OF RICHES

Building Self-Confidence

15 Powerful Stories to Ignite
Your Self-Belief

A Journey of Riches – Building Self-Confidence
15 Powerful Stories to Ignite Your Self-Belief

Published by Motion Media International
Editors: Eric Wyman, Yasmin Phillip, Parker Hansen, Rosemary Lawton and Arynne Priest
Cover Design: Motion Media International
Typesetting & Assembly: Motion Media International

Printing: Amazon and Ingram Sparks
Creator: John Spender - Primary Author
Title: *A Journey of Riches – Building Self-Confidence*

ISBN Digital: 978-1-925919-87-5
ISBN Print: 978-1-925919-88-2
Subjects: Motivation, Inspiration, Memoir

ACKNOWLEDGMENTS

R eading and writing are gifts that very few give to themselves. It is such a powerful way to reflect and gain closure from the past; reading and writing are therapeutic processes. The experience raises one's self-esteem, confidence, and awareness of self.

I learned this when I collated the first book in the *A Journey of Riches* series, which now includes forty books with over 400 co-authors from over 50 countries. Writing about your personal experiences is difficult, and I honor and respect every author who has collaborated in the series.

For many authors, English is their second language, which is a significant achievement. In creating this anthology of short stories, I have been touched by the generosity, gratitude, and shared energy this experience has given everyone.

The inspiration for *A Journey of Riches: Building Self-Confidence* was born from my desire to share empowering stories that ignite the self-confidence within us all. Each chapter is written by a different author, each offering their unique wisdom on the transformative power of growth, resilience, and self-belief.

Each author explores the many facets of personal development, from overcoming self-doubt to embracing challenges as opportunities for growth. Through their stories, insights, and experiences, this book guides you on a journey of empowerment, encouraging you to tap into their inner strength and cultivate lasting confidence. Together, these voices illuminate the path to living life

Acknowledgments

to the fullest, teaching that self-confidence is not a destination, but an ongoing journey fueled by courage, perseverance, and a commitment to continuous growth.

I want to thank all the authors for entrusting me with their unique memories, encounters, and wisdom. Thank you for sharing and opening the door to your soul so others may learn from your experience. I trust the readers will gain confidence from your successes and wisdom from your failures.

I also want to thank my family. I know you are proud of me, seeing how far I have come from that ten-year-old boy learning to read and write at a basic level. So big shout out to Mom, Robert, Dad, and Merril; my brother Adam and his daughter Krystal; my sister Hollie and her partner Brian; my nephew Charlie and niece, Heidi; thank you for your support. Also to my grandparents, Gran and Pop, and Ma and Pa, who now rest in peace. They accept me just as I am with all my travels and adventures worldwide.

Thanks to the team at Motion Media International; you have done an excellent job editing and collating this book. It was a pleasure working with you on this successful project, and I thank you for your patience in dealing with the changes and adjustments along the way.

Thank you, the reader, for having the courage to examine your life and consider how you can improve your future in a rapidly changing world.

Again, thank you to my co-authors: **Linda Orr-Easo, Kim Frazer, Oksana Aya, Kelly Graver, Heather Price, Kristen Dolan, Emeryelle Moore, Joanne Mengwasser, Harita Gandhi-**

Kashyap, Emily Moon, James Greenshields, Leith Alayne, Julian Mann, and John Kelly.

With gratitude,
John R. Spender

TABLE OF CONTENTS

Praise for *A Journey of Riches Book Series*

—⊷o⟡o⊶—

"The *A Journey of Riches* book series is a great collection of inspiring short stories that will leave you wanting more!"
~ Alex Hoffmann, Network Marketing Guru

"If you are looking for an inspiring read to get you through any change, this is it! This book comprises many gripping perspectives from a collection of successful international authors with a tone of wisdom to share."
~ Theera Phetmalaigul, Entrepreneur/Investor

"*A Journey of Riches* is an empowering series that implements two simple words for overcoming life's struggles.

By diving into the meaning of the words 'problem' and 'challenge,' you will be motivated to believe in the triumph of perseverance. With many different authors from all around the world coming together to share various stories of life's trials, you will find yourself drenched in encouragement to push through even the darkest of battles. The stories are heartfelt personal shares of moving through and transforming challenges into rich life experiences.

The book will move, touch, and inspire your spirit to face and overcome life's adversities. It is a truly inspirational read. Thank you for being the kind, open soul you are, John!"
~ Casey Plouffe, Seven Figure Network Marketer

"A must-read for anyone facing major changes or challenges in life right now. This book will give you the courage to overcome any struggle with confidence, grace, and ease."
~ Jo-Anne Irwin, Transformational Coach and Best-Selling Author

"I have enjoyed the *A Journey of Riches* book series. Each person's story is written from the heart, and everyone's journey is different. However, we all have a story to tell, and John Spender does an amazing job of finding authors and combining their stories into uplifting books."
~ Liz Misner Palmer, Foreign Service Officer

"A timely read as I'm facing a few challenges right now. I like the various insights from the different authors. This book will inspire you to move through any challenge or change you are experiencing."
~ David Ostrand, Business Owner

"I've known John Spender for a while now, and I was blessed with an opportunity to be in book four in the series. I know that you will enjoy this new journey, like the rest of the books in the series. The collection of stories will assist you with making changes, dealing with challenges, and seeing that transformation is possible for your life."
~ Charlie O'Shea, Entrepreneur

"The *A Journey of Riches* series will draw you in and help you dig deep into your soul. These authors have unbelievable life stories of purpose inside of them. John Spender is dedicated to bringing peace, love, and adventure to the world of his readers! Dive into this series, and you will be transformed!"
~ Jeana Matichak, Author of *Finding Peace*

"Awesome! Truly inspirational! It is amazing what the human spirit can achieve and overcome! Highly recommended!"
~ Fabrice Beliard, Australian Business Coach and Best-Selling Author

"The *A Journey of Riches* series is a must-read. It is an empowering collection of inspirational and moving stories full of courage, strength, and heart. Bringing peace and awareness to those lucky enough to read to assist and inspire them on their life journey."
~ Gemma Castiglia, Avalon Healing, Best Selling Author

"The *A Journey of Riches* book series is an inspirational collection of books that will empower you to take on any challenge or change in life."
~ Kay Newton, Midlife Stress Buster, and Best-Selling Author

"The *A Journey of Riches* book series is an inspiring collection of stories, sharing many different ideas and perspectives on how to overcome challenges, deal with change, and make empowering choices in your life. Open the book anywhere and let your mood choose where you need to read. Buy one of the books today; you'll be glad that you did!"
~ Trish Rock, Modern Day Intuitive, Best-Selling Author, Speaker, Psychic & Holistic Coach

"*A Journey of Riches* is another inspiring read. The authors are from all over the world, and each has a unique perspective to share that will have you thinking differently about your current circumstances in life. An insightful read!"
~ Alexandria Calamel, Success Coach and Best-Selling Author

Praise for A Journey of Riches Book Series

"The *A Journey of Riches* book series is a collection of real-life stories, which are truly inspiring and give you the confidence that no matter what you are dealing with in your life, there is a light at the end of the tunnel and a very bright one at that. Totally empowering!"
~ John Abbott, Freedom Entrepreneur

"An amazing collection of true stories from individuals who have overcome great changes and who have transformed their lives and used their experience to uplift, inspire, and support others."
~ Carol Williams, Author, Speaker & Coach

"You can empower yourself from the power within this book that can help awaken the sleeping giant within you. John has a purpose in life to bring inspiring people together to share their wisdom for the benefit of all who venture deep into this book series. If you are looking for inspiration to be someone special, this book can be your guide."
~ Bill Bilwani, Renowned Melbourne Restaurateur

"In the *A Journey of Riches* series, you will catch the impulse to step up, reconsider, and settle for only the very best for yourself and those around you. Penned from the heart and with an unflinching drive to make a difference for the good of all, the *A Journey of Riches* series is a must-read."
~ Steve Coleman, author of *Decisions, Decisions! How to Make the Right One Every Time*

"Do you want to be on top of your game? *A Journey of Riches* is a must-read with breakthrough insights that will help you do just that!"
~ Christopher Chen, Entrepreneur

"In *A Journey of Riches*, you will find the insight, resources, and tools you need to transform your life. By reading the author's stories, you, too, can be inspired to achieve your greatest accomplishments and what is truly possible for you. Reading this book activates your true potential for transforming your life way beyond what you think is possible. Read it and learn how you, too, can have a magical life."
~ Elaine Mc Guinness, Best Selling Author of *Unleash Your Authentic Self!*

"If you are looking for an inspiring read, look no further than the *A Journey of Riches* book series. The books are an inspiring collection of short stories that will encourage you to embrace life even more. I highly recommend you read one of the books today!"
~ Kara Dono, Doula, Healer, and Best-Selling Author

"The *A Journey of Riches* book series is filled with real-life short stories of heartfelt tribulations turned into uplifting self-transformation by the power of the human spirit to overcome adversity. The journeys captured in these books will encourage you to embrace life in a whole new way. I highly recommend reading this inspiring anthology series."
~ Chris Drabenstott, Best Selling Author and Editor

"There is so much motivational power in the *A Journey of Riches* series!! Each book is a compilation of inspiring, real-life stories by several different authors, which makes the journey feel more relatable and success more attainable. If you are looking for something to move you forward, you'll find it in one (or all) of these books."
~ Cary MacArthur, Personal Empowerment Coach

"I've been fortunate to write with John Spender, and now, I call him a friend. The *A Journey of Riches* book series features real stories that have inspired me and will inspire you. John has a passion for finding amazing people from all over the world, giving the series a global perspective on relevant subject matters."
~ Mike Campbell, Fat Guy Diary, LLC

"The *A Journey of Riches* series is the reflection of beautiful souls who have discovered the fire within. Each story takes you inside the truth of what truly matters in life. While reading these stories, my heart space expanded to understand that our most significant contribution in this lifetime is to give and receive love. May you also feel inspired as you read this book."
~ Katie Neubaum, Author of *Transformation Calling*

"*A Journey of Riches* is an inspiring testament that love and gratitude are the secret ingredients to living a happy and fulfilling life. This series is sure to inspire and bless your life in a big way. Truly an inspirational read that is written and created by real people, sharing real-life stories about the power and courage of the human spirit."
~ Jen Valadez, Emotional Intuitive and Best-Selling Author

"If you are looking for an inspirational read, look no further than the *A Journey of Riches* book series. The books are an inspiring and educational collection of short stories from the author's soul that will encourage you to embrace life even more. I've even given them to my clients, too, so that their journeys inspire them in life for wealth, health, and everything else in between. I recommend you make it a priority to read one of the books today!"
~ Goro Gupta, Chief Education Officer, Mortgage Terminator, Property Mentor

PREFACE

I collated this book by carefully selecting authors from around the world, each of whom generously shares their personal experiences and reflections on what "Building Self-Confidence" truly means to them. This book represents the collective wisdom of these diverse voices, offering a rich tapestry of perspectives on how self-confidence is nurtured, challenged, and ultimately cultivated through life's unique experiences.

Each author brings a distinct story, illustrating the diverse paths to empowerment, resilience, and growth. Together, these narratives serve as a powerful reminder that building self-confidence is not a one-size-fits-all journey, but rather a deeply personal and evolving process shaped by challenges, triumphs, and everything in between.

Storytelling is how humankind communicates ideas and learns throughout our civilization. While we have become more sophisticated with technology and life in the modern world is now more convenient, there is still much discontent and dissatisfaction. Many people have also moved away from reading books and are missing valuable information that can help them move forward with a positive outlook. Moving toward the tasks or dreams that scare us breeds confidence in growing towards becoming better versions of ourselves.

I think it is essential to turn off the television, slow down, read, reflect, and take the time to appreciate everything you have in life. Start with an anthology book as it offers a cornucopia of viewpoints relating to a particular theme. Here, it's fear and how others have dealt with it. We feel stuck in life or have challenges in a particular area because we see the problem through the same lens that created it. With this compendium and all the books in the *A Journey of Riches* series, you have many writing styles and perspectives that will help you think and see your challenges differently, motivating you to elevate your circumstances.

Anthology books are also great because you can start from any chapter and gain valuable insight or a nugget of wisdom without the feeling that you have missed something from earlier chapters.

I love reading many personal development books because learning and personal growth are vital. If you are not learning and growing, you're staying the same. Everything in the universe is growing, expanding, and changing. If we are not open to different ideas and ways to think and be, then even the most skilled and educated can become closed-minded.

This book series aims to open you up to diverse ways of perceiving your reality. It encourages and gives you many avenues of thinking about the same subject. I wish for you to feel empowered to make a decision that will best suit you in moving forward with your life. As Albert Einstein said, **"We cannot solve problems with the same level of thinking that created them."** So, with Einstein's words in mind, let your mood pick a chapter, or read from the beginning to the end and be guided to find the answers you seek.

With gratitude,
John R. Spender

"You gain strength, courage, and confidence by every experience in which you really stop to look fear in the face."

~ Eleanor Roosevelt

CHAPTER ONE

---∽○❧∾○⊱---

The Alchemy of Confidence: Transforming Experience into Self-Mastery

By James Greenshields

"**C**onfidence requires one to cultivate the ability to receive as well as to give."

A measure of a person's self-confidence is their capacity to be comfortable in the unknown. For we do not fear the unknown; we fear we cannot survive in it. Therefore, to be comfortable, I must truly know myself.

I sit here reflectively in my comfortable armchair, with a freshly brewed cup of tea and a smile on my face. A smile born of witnessing the Divine play itself out in another person trying to find themselves. I've just put the phone down after talking with another mature-aged man asking my advice about whether he should join the military. This is not the first conversation like this, nor will it be the last.

The smile is born of wisdom and the ability to witness the knowledge of what this man seeks, yet he cannot find it even in plain sight. The smile encapsulates a love of humanity that knows this person desires the initiation once instrumental in societies

around the globe, yet this 'civilised society' believes it knows
better. A baptism where he would have what he inherited as his
knowledge of self ripped from his very being. Once this process was
complete, and not before, he would be shown how to build himself
in his own image. Earning confidence in himself.

One's self-confidence will either be linked to internal or external
gauges. If the confidence has been linked to external measures, its
level will have limits determined by those external factors. For
example, if you require external validation from your boss about
your performance so you can feel confident, when it doesn't come,
or comes in a way you were not happy with, your confidence
suffers. Self-confidence built on internal metrics knows no limits.
This man, like most asking these questions, has their confidence tied
to their external world. They require things outside themselves to
provide credibility to their confidence level.

Just listening to this person's level of confidence, the energy behind
their language, and their need to prove themselves capable
demonstrated his confidence metrics were external. In listening
deeply to this person's questions, it was easy to understand the
conversation was not about 'should I join the military?' It was, 'how
do I know when I'm a man? How do I develop confidence in myself
to know I am enough?' He could join the military, or another
intensely testing environment, serve for a while, then leave and still
not have answered the questions he was actually wrestling with. The
conundrum of confidence is that it must be earned, and the gauges
must be internalized.

Confidence is unearthed in experience. Many with knowledge are
not yet wise, for the bridge between knowledge and wisdom is

experiential understanding. In simplistic terms, there are two types of confidence. The first is confidence gained from the mastery of a skill.

I was mentoring the captain of an Australian Rules Football Club. During this time, I would visit him at the club, go to the team meetings and debriefs, and stand on the sidelines during the drills. I enjoyed talking with the other players when, during one such conversation, I quickly became aware he demonstrated underlying low self-confidence. I observed this because I listened to what he was saying between his words and felt his energy during the conversation. There was an undertone of self-doubt. He would add justification to his explanation to elicit acknowledgement. He looked for cues of agreement in me and he talked about the pressure he was experiencing holding his position on the team.

Half an hour later, while watching the drills on the sidelines, the head of leadership development came up for a chat. He was a lovely, engaging person with a lot of credibility from his tremendous personal playing career. The conversation turned to the player with whom I had just been talking. I asked about this player's level of self-confidence and received a quick reply as to him being a very confident young man. So I asked a series of questions: is he at times erratic having great moments followed quickly by flat ones? Does he drop his head and cannot run back into the competition when the ball isn't directed to him, and does he have a level of blaming others? Wide-eyed, the Leadership Coach looked at me and said yes to them all. I smiled and said, that means his confidence is an act, and deep down he's struggling.

In my time working as a leadership mentor to CEOs, the military, and professional athletes amongst others, I've often seen a level of false confidence. You may have heard the statement "fake it until you make it." There is a half-truth to this statement; however, it can also be dangerous. True confidence in your capability comes through dedication to mastering the skill and the ability to create an honest self-feedback loop. This player suffers from what I refer to as high performer syndrome where his self-reflection is judgemental and destructive, instead of balanced and constructive. His inner dialogue was often negative, which caused a natural defensive behaviour of projection onto others, often as blame or judgment.

During the same visit to the club, I attended the club meeting to announce the leadership team for the year. One of the Co-Captains was a man mountain standing over two metres tall. He had a significant presence mixed perfectly with a good level of humility. During his speech, however, I noticed him using a lot of 'ums' and 'ahs.' So many that it distracted from his message. In the psychology of conversation, these little words we put into sentences to fill the gaps are called irritators. They distract the listener and disrupt the transmission of the presenter's message. Later that day, he jogged past me during training. I took the opportunity to congratulate him on his participation in the presentation. He stopped and engaged, so I asked if he would like some feedback, to which he enthusiastically agreed. I mentioned the irritators and how cleaning them up amplifies the power of the message. He thanked me and turned to run off before abruptly stopping and asking, "What's the best way to knock them on the head?" This is an example of a person with a grounded sense of confidence and a proactive approach to personal improvement, encompassing a balanced and constructive feedback loop.

The second type of confidence is deeper, and more universal. It is the confidence in knowing who I am. This level of confidence allows one to enter the unknown, confident in the knowledge of who they are, not requiring to have all the answers, yet possessing a deep inner knowing they will have what it takes to make it in the situation. This level of personal confidence allows for balance within oneself to observe what is going on in a situation. One example was my ability to see the lack of confidence in the AFL player. Another example was during my time as a Combat Team Commander leading over a hundred soldiers in Iraq.

Part of my role in Iraq was as a Senior Coalition Military Commander for the province our Battle Group oversaw. Near the airbase where we were stationed was an area from which we had been rocketed many times. We knew a unit of militia manned the local Police Station, so I made an unannounced visit. I commanded an Australian Cavalry Combat Team using a thirty-eight-wheeled 14-tonne armoured vehicle called an ASLAV. Driving into the police station, I got out, leaving my rifle in the vehicle, with only my pistol in my hip holster.

To the Iraqis, the pistol is a more commanding weapon as it's worn by people in positions of power. I grabbed my nervous interpreter and walked to the front door. A senior policeman met us and asked us to enter. My knowledge of Iraqi religious tradition told me that because I had been invited in, under Sharia Law, I was now under their protection. Within five minutes, I was having 'chai tea' with the station chief and approximately 50 young men crowded into the small room, all armed with machine guns.

The young men in the room were excited young lap dogs whose courage came from the weapons they held and the oversized uniforms they wore. This could be seen at a glance. I engaged the commander politely, asking questions of him and sharing a little about myself. I was bringing a human face to the person they saw as the enemy. As the commander of our forces, I was always treated with respect and displayed a high level of confidence in myself and my capabilities as an Army Officer. Just as the young Iraqi police officer, however, it was a different story when you removed the uniform, weapon, and Armoured Combat Team sitting waiting in support. My confidence was wedded to external metrics.

The path of external requirements, toys, trophies, and accolades to underpin self-confidence was the road the man from the phone call was traveling. Hence the smile for having the experience of becoming master of my craft, only to crash internally for not knowing the answer to the penultimate question: Who Am I?

The crash came within the first year of leaving the military. I found myself collapsed on the couch with my daughters, just having run past me on the way out the door to play fairies. My wife, Kirsty, followed them, full of love and joy. They all loved me so much, yet there I sat, immune to the elation as I was stuck in my hole of self-defeat, judgment, and loathing. The pain I was in because of the build-up of shame and guilt due to my emotional illiteracy left me believing there was no other thing to do—I needed to kill myself. I needed to leave so they could be free of them and me and the pain I thought I brought. As I was about to move to bring the finale, a memory of my father came to me.

I was eight and had just finished feeding a mob of Angus cattle out the back of our property. The Ute had come to a stop with my father and me on the back. There stood this immense figure I called Dad; a farmer, a priest, Chaplain to the Army, Police, and Fire Brigade, and a veteran of the Vietnam Conflict. Confidently gazing off into a part of the bush, I feared. It was an incredibly powerful place, and I had found Aboriginal artifacts there several years earlier. The fear came because I didn't have an elder to take me into the country and show me how to connect. Fear comes from disconnection.

Suddenly, without looking at me, Dad made a sweeping gesture with his hand across the bush to our front and said, "There's my god." Confused, as this did not fit the conservative Christian narrative I was taught at school, I simply watched him. After a moment, he turned and looked deep into my eyes, as if not talking to me directly, but something deeper inside and said, "But you must find your own."

These words erupted from within as if from the very part of my soul my Father spoke to that day. The message was clear. I hadn't done everything I was meant to in this life. I needed to find my god, my connection to the Divine, or, as some will say, the Great Spirit. And then, as if symbols were being lined up in front of me in my darkest hour, I remembered the words of Viktor Frankl in his epic book of human understanding, *Man's Search for Meaning*, when he said, "Suffering ceases to be suffering when meaning is found." My path was clear. I was now on a mission to heal and find meaning.

Whenever I engage in a conversation about confidence, like this man asking about joining the military, I find they do not have deep meaning in their life. If there is, they do not feel like it has been earned. If I am to embody confidence, I must believe I have been tested and it has been earned. Now here lies the trap. Many, if they could see themselves through the eyes of loved ones or respected peers, have already earned this right, yet refuse to allow themselves to receive through acknowledgement. The underlying issue here is their core psychological wound of I am not enough.

Sipping my tea, the smile of reflection deepens as I think back on my journey to break through the not-enough wound and transcend it to a place of: I Am. My path of ownership and earning my confidence required me to experience the moment in time when I was going to take my life. Where the metrics needed to fail completely so I could learn another way: the internal.

The collapse occurred because I had become so ingrained in the inherited beliefs of what everyone else thought I should be, how I should act, and what I needed to achieve for success, that I had completely lost the connection to myself I had as a young child. I needed my entire life to collapse and dissolve, for everything I once knew to be true or fact to disintegrate. In mythological terms, the Grand Illusion known as the Veil of Isis by some, or *Maya* by others, or the biblical temple curtain needed to be split from top to bottom, so I could see truly once again.

The ancient Chinese would always build the place of healing at the summit of many, many steps. This brought the seeker to their knees; to dissolve the ego and allow healing to begin. On that day, when I sat on the couch in pain, I was finally on my knees. I find it so interesting that the etymology of Apocalypse is "a great unveiling," taken from 14th-century Greek. To put all of this another way, the collapse of my life as I knew it was the start of my true initiation into the deepest connection with myself. From which the foundation of confidence springs.

I joined the military straight out of Boarding School. Two great institutions are famous for their initiations. What I didn't realize at the time was they were false initiations. The process of a rite of passage or an initiation is to break the person down. To set them free of what they inherited as a belief system about themselves, what they thought were their safe places, so they can be rebuilt with a new identity. A false initiation occurs when the institution or tribe rebuilds the person in the way they desire for their purposes and the identity is tied to the tribe or institution. The person, therefore, requires that construct to know who they are. Therefore, so many people struggle when leaving heavily structured organisations such as the military, police, emergency services, medicine, education, and professional sports to name but a few.

A true initiation is when the person, after dissolving, is shown the path to rebuild themselves from the inside out. This breeds a grounded sense of self-confidence in the individual and gives the tribe the knowledge of the initiates' capabilities. A special person can go through a false initiation, yet because of a deep connection to self, maintain their own identity. These are rare and powerful people. I was not one of them.

As I sit here thinking of initiations, my mind jumps to my experiences deep in the jungles of Kalimantan, which I visited some four years after my darkest day sitting on the couch. The soul-searching work I had done within myself over those four years took me to places I was more scared of than the battlefield. At least I had been trained for combat. The outcome of this journey, however, was demonstrated dramatically on this expedition.

Kalimantan is the largest Indonesian island with the oldest rainforest in the world, known as the third largest set of lungs on the planet. Unfortunately, due to greed and a consumptive-based paradigm, these lungs are quickly being destroyed. I remember my time with the elders of an indigenous tribe, the Kenyah Dayak, a people who are truly connected to the old initiations. I took part in an expedition to help them visit their ancient ancestral burial caves. None, bar the Shaman had seen them and he was just six years old when he left his mother, family, and village. In the 1960's, their people moved from these original lands deep in the forest, to a more accessible location adhering to the advice of Christian Missionaries who said they needed better access to modern medicine and education and this Shaman in the making went with them.

The Dayak trek was the first time I had been in the jungle without a map, compass, or GPS. My connection to these people, the one named Ramon, was incredible. To witness their ease of movement, keen eye, and connection to the environment was awe-inspiring. My comfort in the bush was born of growing up on a central Victorian sheep and cattle farm of just over 2000 acres. This comfort was then honed with 17 years in the military in a frontline Cavalry Unit. After my service, I returned to live in the bush running retreats and rites of passage programs.

Moving alongside Ramon, it was easy to see he was an initiated person. His confidence in his own abilities was incorruptible. He oozed credibility with his quiet, can-do, proactive nature that saw him always looking where he could be of the best service. I held the

12-gauge shotgun he had hand-crafted with excellence. The machining done in a local village with limited tools was precise. I asked him if he would take me hunting, to which he agreed.

When the time came for the hunt, it was evening and a tropical storm began. A large part of me didn't want to go because of the rain; however, the other part of my mind strongly explained this was a once-in-a-lifetime opportunity and I was to get off my wet bum and go ask if Ramon was ready. Talking through an interpreter, Ardi, I got a sense of hesitancy in Ramon about going. When I pressed the issue with Ardi, he told me Ramon would take me if I wanted to go. I responded by asking: what does Ramon want? Ramon saw no point in the hunt, as we were moving on in the morning and the kill would have to be left behind. I smiled deeply at this connected man who would only lift his power to the service of something greater with no need to prove himself by taking life unnecessarily. I thanked Ramon and Ardi and returned to my sleep site.

The highlight of the expedition, and the point where I truly saw who I had become as a person, was when I stood in the open mouth of a natural cave 100 metres above the rainforest canopy. This cave was in a limestone escarpment that ran as far as you could see in both directions and was full of sarcophagi from the tribal elders, dating back hundreds of years. I stood there, honored to be the first white man to set foot on this ledge.

The feeling of the place was so intense that tears consumed me. The Dayak bounced around me like kids in a candy shop, obviously in an altered state of consciousness induced by nothing but the space itself. A deep desire to jump overcame me as I stood there on the ledge. This wasn't a suicidal thought at all. Instead, it was born of this deep connection to everything and an intense feeling of freedom. In an instant, my thoughts were grabbed by images of my wife and our two daughters. As quickly as they came, I was met by the message. They are completely okay and completely capable of living their best life. I realized I was now complete. I knew who I was and had come to a place of humble ownership.

Standing on the cliff's edge brought me into unity with both life and death. An inner fulfilment to a quest I'd unknowingly been on my entire life. The closing of one chapter and the opening of the next: living this unfolded version of myself. The experience of living life this way allowed me to exercise my newfound internalized confidence when I had no external understanding. What better example could I ask for than being a father? A role where part of the job description is to set the platform for your children to develop their understanding of self and from that place, nurture a grounded sense of self-confidence.

Part of being a father is to hold space for your children to rebel against you in creating their own identity; truly earning and owning the story of who they are. When both our daughters were in their early teenage years, Kirsty and I told them they needed to rebel. To find their path and to become capable of making their own decisions in life. Just because their mother and I did things one way, did not mean it was the way right for them. They needed to find the path to their inner decision-maker, their inner Queen. We talked about the two ways to rebel, either actively or passively. It was their choice which path they took.

Our eldest, Abigail, is a powerful young woman who has had trouble owning this aspect of herself. About six months into the rebellion, she and I were on a road trip when I asked how the rebellion was going for her. The stony silence was epic. So after a few minutes, I offered: the authority you are rebelling against always dictates the rebellion. If the authority moves, the rebel must go the other way. The power remains with the authority. Even if the rebel was to win, they simply became that which they fought so hard to bring down. The son becoming the father, the victim becoming the victimiser, the invalidated one doing the invalidation.

When I asked Abigail what the purpose of the rebellion was in the first place, she immediately answered—" to own who I truly am." I felt immense love for her at that point and offered, "You can always set the rebellion aside and simply own your identity." To this day, I am truly honored to witness both girls crafting their own stories, forging their identities, and earning their confidence.

One of the greatest gifts has come in situations where I have allowed the witnessing of my daughters forging their path to become hard and stressful. Put another way, I have allowed myself to become emotionally triggered when they did things with which I would disagree. In these times I have realized I generally put an attachment on the method or outcome being a certain way. This attachment causes a perspective that brings tension and with it, pain. Pain is a contractive emotion, such as anger, sadness, fear, shame, or guilt. From which, if I acted, the behaviour would create turbulence in our relationship.

I have found great wisdom regarding the topic of attachment in the teaching of a man I would describe as the best psychologist to ever walk the planet: Siddhartha Gautama, otherwise known as Lord Buddha. The Noble Truths of Buddhism teach the concept of Dukkha, or suffering. Attachment brought that suffering on, be that a craving or an aversion. To release suffering, one need only release the attachment.

The pain of attachment during witnessing is a signal that I have made the situation about myself and am not allowing myself to truly see my daughters. That means I cannot truly be of service to them as my vision is clouded by emotion triggered by my need, not theirs. I have come to a place where I simply ask: What is the greatest possible intention for this situation? Put in a spiritual context, what is the Divine's greatest intention for me at this moment? These questions, whether phrased psychologically or spiritually, provide an opportunity to transcend the situation, causing pain in the moment, by opening my mind to the possible higher-level meaning. Meaning can then provide context and allow the situation to fit into the greater purpose. Again, I am brought back to Viktor Frankl's statement about suffering and meaning.

The second key reason for my ability to hold space for my loved ones is that I am no longer attached to what they think of me. Their love doesn't define my identity. This means I can truly love them as I'm not attached to a need to be seen in a certain way for me to receive their love. I know in my heart they love me, and that is all I need. I also know that, when speaking, I must speak in truth. They know not to ask a question of me for which they are not ready to hear the answer. This places power squarely in each one of us in the relationship. It means I have crafted a place where I can just be me, authentically, confidently, warts and all. I've reached a point where

I've replaced self-judgment with honest appraisal and a desire to grow.

All emotions have a message for us. All emotions are healthy, including anger, sadness, fear, shame, and guilt. These five, however, are the ones we suppress because of emotional illiteracy. Befriending them, sitting in them, alchemizing them into their purest version, and listening to the messages they have for us, sets us free.

A confident person assists others to excel, not at their own expense, but in a deep strength of confidence that knows they are enough and helping others will yield a better result. This has been the place I have learned to look at fatherhood.

As my cup of tea ends, the smile of contentment is complete. I needed to be the equivalent of the young Iraqi policemen. Nothing in my path has been out of place or superfluous. Everything has gone into this journey of building the confident, capable, and credible individual I am today. I no longer need external recognition, yet I enjoy being humble and gracious in receiving it when it comes.

So, my challenge to you as the reader is to reflect on your initiations. Were they false or pure? Were they complete or is part of the journey still left to tread? You will know not when your head tells you, but when you feel comfortable in your skin, comfortable to just be you.

"Self-confidence is a superpower. Once you start believing in yourself, magic starts happening."

~ Unknown

CHAPTER TWO

From Fear to Fun through Faith

By Linda Orr-Easo

W hen I think back to when I was young—yes, my memory does go back that far—my first images and memories are of a small, shy girl who came into this life with a deep desire to be there for others, and who depended on others to reassure her she was "good enough."

Little did I know that this one element, i.e., reassurance from others, would become one of the main reasons I found it so difficult for many years to really feel confident in myself.

Thankfully, this shy young girl has become a confident, not-so-young woman.

If this chapter can help you open up to the beautiful, powerful person that you are, then I am truly grateful for this opportunity to share.

In hindsight, I have recognized the fact that my personal growth has evolved in two main phases:

- What I do

- Who I am

And, I have realized the link between the two.

It was in my late thirties that building my self-confidence began—at least in concrete terms, as I am aware that each experience we have in life is an opportunity to grow. Where I was working, I was offered the chance to be coached by a wonderful, wise man.

His name was Pierre. One lesson was: "If you don't make mistakes, how do you know what you don't know? How do you progress?" This made perfect sense to me, and with his caring coaching, I gradually started smiling when I made mistakes and was grateful for the opportunity to learn. Of course, it depended on the importance of the mistake.

I then trained to be a coach, and my first one-on-one session was a disaster. The person who had been in one of my training courses had come to me for help. I listened as she shared her professional issues, which quickly veered into her personal problems. She started crying, and her story was objectively sad. I started crying too, and we shared the box of tissues.

As soon as I walked out of this session, I was ashamed of myself. I had just jumped into a deep hole with the other person, and I'd "reassured" her of how bad her situation was. My self-confidence professionally hit a new low. I felt really upset, as this was a direction I had hoped to move more into.

I immediately called Pierre, and his words of wisdom again resonated.

1. What did you learn from this experience?

2. If she comes back and asks to see you again, what will you do?

She did, in fact, come back, and it went significantly better.

Looking back, this moment had a significant impact on me by opening me to and helping me accept my mistakes and feeling grateful for the lessons they brought.

Of course, being a perfectionist didn't exactly help me. Even when others told me that something I was doing was good, if I saw even a small area for improvement, I couldn't let go of the work until I resolved that "problem."

This personality trait also meant that I was afraid of making mistakes. I finally understood that behind this was the fear that mistakes would disappoint others and would change their high opinion of me.

As I then no longer feared making mistakes, I was open to trying out new skills and new ways of doing things, both in my professional and personal life. I can't say that I looked forward to making mistakes, but when I did, it often made me smile in gratitude for the opportunity. The more new areas I discovered and tried out, the more confident I felt. At a certain point, it was as if I realized the infinite ways that I could grow. I was no longer limiting myself to hide in my "safe" areas.

I love the quote by Anais Nin:

> "And the day came when the risk of remaining tight in a bud became more painful than the risk it took to blossom."

When I first read this, I felt emotional, as I knew deep down that I was hurting, trying to keep myself closed so that I wouldn't be seen for who I truly was. And yet, somewhere deep within, I knew that I was a good person and, like everyone on this planet, I had my own gifts to share.

I also learned about visualization—creating in my mind's eye the image that I wanted to see. As my job involved presenting and training, it became important to project the professional image that I believed others expected to see and to give a certain level of reassurance to others that being there with me was worth their time.

So, I started seeing myself as I would like others to see me, and of course how I would like to see myself—confident, caring, listening, knowledgeable, etc.

It amazed me how I could switch from one image to another, from one where I felt nervous and reflected this in my image to one where I changed the image and, somehow, magically, I felt calmer. Initially, I felt I was pretending, and yet little by little I could feel and see the difference and how this was helping build my self-confidence.

One particular moment comes to mind. I came into the office and shared that I was nervous about the presentation that I was going to make. The other colleagues assumed I was joking, as they saw me as a confident person who never showed any signs of nervousness. One of the colleagues even felt a bit annoyed that I was pretending to get nervous.

Thinking about this just after, I realized I was halfway there by showing up for others professionally.

Another moment at work was during an annual performance review when my manager pointed out that I was sometimes unclear when I was making a point in a meeting or discussion. And he was right. I call it my Nervous Mumbo-Jumbo. I had the tendency to repeat myself and add lots of extras. First, I started expressing my thoughts and needs more clearly and confidently, which had a positive effect on my self-worth, such as giving me permission to express myself honestly. This involved taking the time to clearly decide on the message or information I wanted to share and then make it simpler, shorter, and deliver it more slowly. I gradually got out of the "repeat it to make it clearer" mode.

Who I Am

As mentioned at the beginning of this article, I am now aware of the two phases of building my self-confidence. The above examples are what I do, and now I would like to share the second phase: who I am.

When I started coaching others, I found it powerful and beautiful when people opened up honestly about what was working and what was not working in their lives. I then saw people more as individuals and less in terms of what they could do.

It was as if, by witnessing this openness in others, which touched my heart, I gave myself permission to do the same.

After all, surely, who the person is, is far more important than what they can do?

When my clients express doubt in themselves or feeling anxious about moving forward, I invite them to reflect on their past successes, no matter how small. Their energy changes when they reconnect to these moments or experiences. They become calmer, happier, more positive. When I have a moment of doubt, I often think back to one of my own successes and smile. It's a real boost in confidence, and I hear the little voice within say, "You can do this."

By embracing positive self-talk, I have moved from situations of self-doubt and low self-confidence to taking that step to move forward, especially when the path ahead is one that I have not yet been down. I also take a moment to reflect to see if there is a message there for me, or perhaps an invitation to find out more information before going ahead. When I sense that this is my "Little Me" saying "hello" or my ego trying to keep me safe, I give thanks for this, and then say something positive and encouraging. For example, "I can't do this" becomes "I can and I am doing this and I am thrilled that I am."

When I first started opening more to spirituality, I initially felt a reluctance to practice such self-talk or even affirmations. It was as if I was being false in some way, until I learned about just how incredibly powerful our words are, and that it is all a question of vibration, of energy. By sending out this affirmation, this vibration, I now understand how this is heard by the universe—the universe that always says "Yes." So, when I say, "I am not confident," here come the situations that I find more than challenging to resonate with the vibration that I have sent out.

However, when I say, "Yes, I can do this," it is as if all the support I need is there, guiding me. There may be that brief twinge inside, and yet the more I say yes to who I am, the easier it gets.

What I have also become more conscious of is that this vibration affects everyone and everything around me, and the message I am sending out is being heard by my whole body, on various levels of my being—physical, emotional, mental, and spiritual.

The more aligned we are with all levels of our being, the truer we are to ourselves, to our soul. Alignment eliminates doubts and worries, making confidence a given. We move from fear to faith. To the knowing that life is for us—always.

In terms of being authentic, of being true to myself, another aspect that came to the fore was when I started sharing my emotions more honestly. Before, I had tried to portray an image of a happy, positive person—always. And now I could be that person and also express other emotions, e.g., sadness, frustration, etc. The title of one book summed it up for me—*Cessez d'etre gentil, soyez vrai* by Thomas d'Ansembourg, which translates as *Stop being kind, be true*. The term "good enough" evolved from "good at doing" to "good at being."

So how can I tell when I am truly being aligned? How can I check to see if I feel confident or not? One extremely powerful way is to listen to our bodies. It was when I became a reiki master and trained as a reflexologist that I opened to the incredible ways that our bodies are always sending us signs to help us become more aligned.

I don't know about you, but whenever I used to feel nervous because of a lack of self-confidence, I would get a tight feeling in my stomach, my breathing would become shallow, and my shoulders and jaws would be tense. Not to mention the increased heart rate.

Now I often simply take a moment to check how my body is. Is it relaxed, or is it tense? If it is tense, I acknowledge this sign and reflect upon what the message is to help me grow. I can then give thanks for this information and consciously relax my body.

When I feel nervous about doing something new or challenging, I will talk to myself in a loving, reassuring way, reminding myself that making mistakes is okay, and that beyond these detours lies that which I wish to experience, to create. I listen to my body to help me know when I am aligned or not.

I say "listen to my body,"; however, it is in fact my soul that is whispering to me, or loudly shouting depending on how reluctant—or stubborn—I may be about listening to the guidance.

Of course, behind all confidence lie the questions:" Am I worthy?" and "Am I loved?" The two questions are closely intertwined. My belief now is that when we can truly answer "Yes" to these questions, there is no longer any doubt about our self-worth, which leads to our self-esteem and our self-confidence.

Say "Yes" and believe it.

On my journey to become more aligned with who I am, one of the important areas for me to look at, and in fact to study again and again, is the area of values.

One of my core values is honesty.

What had been happening before was I valued honesty in others, and I considered myself to be a very honest person, i.e., I would never think of cheating, stealing, lying, etc. However, and this shocked me when I realized it, there was a serious mismatch between this value and how I had been leading my life.

I had been dishonest with myself and the image I had been projecting to others.

How many masks did I wear to hide who I truly was?

And the more I hid, the less confidence I had.

Initially, I believe I was not even aware of the masks I was wearing—some constantly and others depending on the situation.

As I grew increasingly aware of the masks, I consciously let them go. Of course, there were sometimes a few nervous moments, especially regarding other people's reactions, and yet by opening up to who I truly am, and showing the real me to the world, I had self-confidence.

I am so grateful for the following pivotal moment in my life regarding letting go of the masks.

Here is a quote from a reading by Martin Brofman:

You want to be loved as you are
With no judgements, no expectations

But you have changed yourself
To create an image in order to get love

And what is it that would be loved
Would it be the natural you?
Or the image you have created in order to get love

If it is this image that you have created,
This would still not be satisfying
There would still be the feeling that you are not
loved for who you are.

Thanks to the above, I then started integrating the following steps:

1. Am I pretending or am I being true? I ask this question when I find myself in a challenging situation.

2. What if I continue? How will this look? What if I stop pretending? How will this look?

3. What actions can I take? What actions will I take? Action is the key to confidence.

4. Expressing gratitude for this moment to become more of who I am.

There will be moments when I may fall into self-doubt, my imposter moments. Rather than falling into fear, I now know that these are opportunities for me to step forward, to grow.

A recent example of this is when John contacted me about writing a chapter for one of his books. My first reaction was, "This must be a scam, or perhaps he has mistaken me for someone else."

When I was writing the draft of the chapter, I remember feeling nervous when I saw an email from him with his comments. It took me a moment to even open that email, as I half expected to see pages with lots of red lines on it. Ok, so they were blue lines—only joking. It was fine.

I had, at that point, been writing monthly in the Divine CEO magazine and posting on social media. The owner of the magazine invited me to be on a podcast with her. A definite speeding up of my heartbeat at the mere thought. During the podcast, she asked me, "What are your superpowers? What are your gifts?" Dead silence from me. Theoretically, I know that every single person on this Earth has gifts to share. My acceptance of my gifts was still trying to remain elusive.

So, what can stop us from stepping out of this comfort zone, from breaking free?

The first step could be to ask yourself honestly to what extent you have been or are holding yourself back from being all that you can be.

- Is it because you don't feel you are good enough?

- People-pleasing, for whatever reason, including to feel loved, accepted?

- A perceived need to fit in, or at least not to rock the boat?

- You think it will take too much effort and time?

- Past experiences?

- Fear of being seen differently? Of being "found out?"

- Or something else?

For each of the above, we can reframe to nurture our confidence. Here are just a few examples:

- Not good enough? As there is only one source—God, the universe, whatever term feels right—then every one of us comes from this same source, and therefore our very essence is divine. Not sure anyone would argue that the divine is not good enough.

- People-pleasing, to be loved, appreciated? Who is it that would be loved—the real you or the one you are pretending to be?

- A perceived need to fit in? We can fit in and be true to ourselves, depending on whether we try to pretend to be someone else. What if we could just be ourselves and naturally fit in if we so choose?

- Too much time or effort? Says who? What if we could change our thinking in an instant? And of course, we know we can, if we believe we can.

- Past experiences? Does the past determine the future? Really?

- Fear of being seen differently or being "found out?" How much energy, how much internal struggle does it take to hide who you truly are? "Found out?" What if you could be seen—"found out"—for the beautiful person who you are?

At a certain point, from my experience, I felt like a victim, as if I were being held back, and yet the only person holding me back was myself. Thankfully, I don't blame others for my life. After all, whose life is it?

What if it is those limiting beliefs that our soul is asking us to look at and act upon in these situations? We have a wonderful opportunity to grow, to learn, to question. Painful, of course, and yet deep down there is already a sense of liberation, of being free, that is just waiting to be expressed.

Does it feel scary? Do we feel vulnerable? There are easy answers to these.

This is where the dance between the Little Me and the Big Me can be so much fun. We can say "Ok, now I'm going to do this." "Really, are you sure? What if . . . ?"

A practice that I enjoy is observing the conversations between my Little Me and my Big Me, watching these take place as an observer from the helicopter position, i.e., viewing from the ceiling. As I look down, I connect to the feeling within me in both, and this can cause a sense of true compassion for my Little Me, and a powerful feeling of gratitude for knowing that is always there in my Big Me. It is as if the Big Me is there to reassure the Little Me that all is well, that we are always being guided, supported to discover and embrace the divine paths that are there for us. Naturally, the more we trust ourselves, the stronger our self-confidence becomes.

If at any point the Little Me comes up with lots of reasons to stay where we are, we can simply take a few deep breaths and give thanks for all that this version of ourselves is trying to do—to protect us. Then, connect to Big Me and explore in wonder and gratitude for the incredible possibilities that are there in front of us, sometimes just behind the veil that we have put up. We then connect to how this feels. I know I sometimes get carried away and assume that this is already so. At a certain level, it is. Try telling that wall between our kitchen and dining room that it is no longer there, or my hand as I tried to open the door wide, assuming the wall was already gone.

This helps me remember that I have the choice—to live in fear or in faith.

Another important aspect for me in building my self-confidence is opening to what I love doing, to what brings me joy. It can be in these moments that our hearts open wide, and we share our true self with the world—confidently, consciously.

For me, writing has now become one thing I love doing, as well as training and coaching, the common denominator being to help people open to who they truly are, and in doing so, to create and live a joy-filled life.

The more I choose to embrace this part of my journey, the more opportunities I see before me. I have realized the fact that when I am in the flow, it seems as if everything in my life flows so much easier, and in such incredibly creative ways. Perhaps it is because of my way of seeing a wink from the divine that I am on the path that is right for me.

If ever you are in doubt, or simply need some reassurance, all you have to do is to ask for help, for guidance, and it is always there— always. So, you are never alone. When I opened to this, I felt a huge sense of relief.

From my personal journey into building my self-confidence, I believe that there is only one person who can really do this, and that is you—by choosing to be honest with yourself and with everyone else, by choosing to be you.

Others may give you feedback, pay you compliments, or give you suggestions, but their impact will depend on your decision to open up to the truth inside. You are here as a unique expression of the divine, as is each person on this Earth.

What would it feel like to live your truth, to see yourself standing there confidently, calmly, and radiating the joy and love that is there within you?

It all comes from the inside, with a little help from the outside.

Let the fun begin.

"Confidence is preparation. Everything else is beyond your control."

~ Richard Kline

CHAPTER THREE

⟨∘⟨⟩∘⟩

The Inner Rise:
Rising into Confidence through
Love and Trust

By Emily Moon

The Collective is Rising!

A s magnificent souls come to Earth, we never intended to forget our great love for self or for this human experience, but somewhere along the way, many of us forgot. Perhaps we picked up others' (family members, society, teachers, coaches, friends, etc.) beliefs that did not align with our true essence and unintentionally adopted their inner fears and limiting beliefs as our own, all of which have an effect on inner confidence.

However, all of this is shifting as we are in the time of the Great Awakening that many who came before us spoke of and is, without a doubt, here right now! It's a time of the collective rise beyond fear and limiting beliefs, into a remembrance of who we are as souls on Earth and into our great love that exists in us all.

Because so many are continuously choosing to rise above fear and live more from their soul truths, sovereignty, and self-worth, this makes it easier for others to also access this within themselves, as it's a vibration amplified in the collective field. There is a continuous amplification of these higher vibrations of consciousness available for us to tap into, supporting us to live more as our authentic selves and in our self-worth.

Everyone's path is different, of course, but the collective support is here for you in your own inner rise: the stories, the modalities, the people, the guides, the teachers, the books, the music, the podcasts, the classes, etc. The reference points are all in place to help amplify, support, and usher in this incredible time for humanity's awakening! And it is all being anchored in through great levels of Love, including a deep love for self, which is an essential pillar in building self-confidence.

My Great Awakening and Inner Rise in Self-Confidence

It truly wasn't until I began deeply loving myself that a confidence I never knew could exist within me began to rise.

As a child and before I was more influenced by societal conditioning, I was deeply connected to my innate true essence, but somewhere along the way, I abandoned this inner knowing—this great inner love for myself. I became entangled in the density and forgot who I was. I struggled deeply with not feeling "good enough." I adopted family members' beliefs, sports coaches' expectations, and society's "accepted" ways of living (and many limiting beliefs) as my own. I felt insecure in my own body, enjoyed using alcohol and drugs as access to an unhealthy false inner confidence, and searched for love and validation outside of myself to fill this inner void.

Following college and some big events in my life, including a near-death experience with extensive injuries and the loss of a job, I struggled with bouts of major depression and going on and off antidepressants for almost a decade.

By 2016, at 32, I was married, had a good career, and owned a home. On the outside, my life may have appeared fairly "normal." But on the inside, I didn't feel True happiness. I didn't really know what loving myself felt like. I didn't know the real me I had been searching for—my soul me. And I was far from feeling true confidence.

Always looking for greater meaning to things, I knew deep down there had to be more than "this" life I was experiencing. I just didn't know what that meant... yet!

It was in 2016 that I empowered myself to get off the antidepressants once and for all and started asking bigger questions about life that I couldn't shake, such as:

"Who am I? Why am I here? What is the greater purpose?"

From this constant deep inquiry, things began to rattle inside. A huge internal shift began to take place—a spiritual awakening into deep self-discovery of the True me unfolded fast. A deep remembrance of my true essence was activated as an entirely new dimensional reality unfolded within!

Slowly, but also not so slowly, the answers from a higher power (source, my higher self, my team of angels, my guides) poured in with so much truth and so much love within. It was an activation of deep inner knowing of the magnificent soul of limitless love, light, and potential that I am. That we all are! To put into words this inner remembrance would be limiting. And 2016 was the divine time I chose for my awakening to this inner greatness! My depression fully healed.

My intuition turned on big time and I began receiving divine messages regularly. Everything in my reality was being seen from a higher perspective. More and more parts of me were coming home to my great inner love and I was falling madly in love with myself! And from where I had been operating for so long before, I didn't think that was possible!

No one understood what I was experiencing, but it didn't matter as this unwavering love for self became a priority in my life above all else, which elevated my confidence like never before. And it was just the beginning of a new lens through which to experience life.

Confidence is not about achievement, success, outside validation, or how others perceive us. In my eyes, it has everything to do with our love for self and living unapologetically as our true essence. It includes allowing ourselves to be our authentic selves even with those who do not get you!

Within a short time, big shifts and transitions were taking place in my life, including ending my marriage and making a deep, soul-inspired international solo move from Virginia (where I was born and raised and had lived all my life), to the Andes mountains in Cusco, Peru. I hired and trained a small support team, ran my medical device territory remotely, and flew into Virginia as guided. I didn't even question if it would all "work out," I just knew it would in its divine unfoldment. These were just some of the many shifts taking place during this profound time in my life.

And all of it required so much Trust in listening to my heart and oh so much courage. I trusted my soul's guidance, choosing love for me, and taking big-time, inspired action and quantum leaps that catapulted me into an entirely new reality. A newfound confidence I didn't know could exist within me was being embodied like never before in ways I never knew possible and my Soul was leading the way.

Challenging conversations with those who doubted me became experiences I had called into my reality to rise in my inner confidence and celebrate myself even more! I was choosing behaviors, actions, choices, and decisions aligned with a deep appreciation for who I was, grounded in loving and trusting myself more, which are all building blocks of confidence. Something I will be expanding on later in the chapter and offering practices to help you integrate more into your own life!

My inner shift towards living a more confident life was quite a journey. I hold great reverence and gratitude for the past struggles and challenges I experienced, including the lowest of lows, as they led me to intensely seek greater meaning in life, sparking my spiritual awakening into this great love within. Sometimes I would still hit a wall with my thoughts or have an experience where an old version of fear would come back. But my love for self won every single time, still does, and forever will!

I know with absolute certainty, if I was able to rise up, I know it is possible for anyone.

When we courageously move beyond fear and separation and instead choose to live in our authentic soul truth and in our trust and love for self, it's inevitable for confidence to thrive within!

Implementing Self-Love and Self-Trust to Embody Self-Confidence

If you ask me what self-confidence means, from my perspective, it is coming home to the true You, to the deep love for you that you inherently have within, to the absolute birthright of your Worth as a magnificent soul come to Earth!

I know without hesitation that no matter where we are on our paths in life, we can absolutely bridge this coming home to self.

So the questions then arise...

How can we come home to self more?
How can we build more love for self?
How can we build more courage to be authentically ourselves?
How can we build more confidence in self?

In my personal experience and witnessed with countless clients and others, confidence is an inner practice that builds within as we embody more of the truth of who we are through our choices, behaviors, and actions aligned with love for self and our inner truths.

And when we are truly living from this place of self-love and trust, our confidence can't help but coexist alongside this feeling. Almost like a byproduct of the inherent essence of who we are, all stemming from the foundation.

Yes, it's a journey—your unique journey.
Yes, it may take time.
And yes, it requires courage.

But we didn't come here to half love ourselves, to half be into liberating ourselves, to half trust in self. We came here to fully step into our Power of the love we hold inside for ourselves as the magnificent souls on Earth that we are!

And truly, the time is now. There has never been a greater time on our planet to fully step into this deep knowing of who we are and live it.

So, what are some practical ways we can build and grow this more within ourselves?

I will share thoughts and self-inquiry prompts on building this for yourself. I encourage you to write on these pages, add ideas, draw, express yourself, take what resonates, and leave what doesn't. Embody you!

As I mentioned before, self-confidence is an inner practice that builds through our choices, behaviors, and actions aligned with love for self. So, having a deeper awareness of what this looks like for each of us is incredibly helpful. Of course, this will be different for each one of us and our unique journey, but I will offer ways of implementing this more into your everyday life.

Building More Love for Self

When you choose you, you are choosing love for you. By choosing love for yourself, you are living in a place where you are worthy, where you value, appreciate, and honor you. This is all part of embodying self-confidence.

I appreciate myself.
I value myself.
I am worthy.
I love myself.

Self Inquiry: What behaviors and choices support the above phrases that you'd like to incorporate more into your life?

Allow yourself a moment to sit with this, consider how this applies to your life right now, and see what comes through. The invitation is to write your ideas down or perhaps circle the examples below that resonate.

- creating more space just for you, "me time."

- saying yes more to the things that excite you.

- living unapologetically in your authenticity.

- saying no to experiences that do not align with your values.

- speaking your truth more.

- listening to your inner voice more.

- staying hydrated and nourishing your body.

- saying I love you to your precious body more.

- moving on from a job that has not felt good for you in a long time.

- honoring your needs.

- honoring your time to rest and slow down vs. go go go.

- voicing your boundaries to others.

- being more clear with others on what is a yes or no for you regardless of their response.

- sharing your truth in a certain relationship.

- choosing to share your time and energy with people who you feel good around.

- receiving compliments more vs denying it. (i.e., thank you vs who me?)

- allowing yourself to receive help when offered.

- standing up for yourself.

- making choices based on your inner truth and not the truth of others.

- allowing yourself to let go of a relationship that has reached its completion with love for how each served their divine purpose for one another vs holding on to the attachment.

- putting yourself first; a.k.a., filling your cup first.

- taking yourself out on dates.

- writing love notes to yourself and putting them in places to find later.

- allowing yourself to cry it out when needed.

- journaling.

- spending time in nature.

- creating a sacred morning or evening practice just for you.

Perhaps you write out three that are most resonant to your heart at this time and put them in your phone notes or hang them on your fridge as reminders of self-love behaviors you desire to implement more into your life.

By choosing loving behaviors and choices such as these more in your daily life, you are saying yes to yourself, loving yourself, and valuing how important you are. This is a huge inner shift into embodying more self-confidence.

May this section also be received as words of encouragement to allow yourself to make choices beyond those places of self-doubt or fear. Offering them great reverence and gratitude for trying to "protect" you as you bring them into a warm embrace of Love to be set free and, perhaps, once and for all!

As you keep choosing you, watering and nourishing you, your love within will wildly flourish and a new you anchored in self-love can blossom more freely. As you courageously continue choosing Love for yourself, you are truly embodying Confidence! And if others don't recognize the new you, that's perfect. You are showing them what is possible

Building More Trust in Self

Much of our connection to our inner confidence is trusting ourselves, which is a form of deep self-love and includes listening to our inner voice and our heart. Being able to truly listen to our self is such an incredibly empowering place to be.

But how do we get to that place?

Continuously taking inspired action is one of the fastest ways to build trust in yourself and an inner muscle we can build. Inspired action goes beyond thinking, dreaming, or talking about something. It's putting into action what is calling you forward. It's saying yes to that opportunity. It's signing up for that training, workshop, or retreat that is calling you. It's submitting your application for an exciting new job or booking that trip to Italy you always dreamed of! Ultimately, it's listening to your inner voice, your heart or inner excitement through taking action: a decision, choice, behavior, or movement forward. And each inspired action builds an increased sense of confidence.

For example, I could have easily declined the opportunity to co-author this inspiring book, but I listened to my heart and inner excitement guiding me, took inspired action, and said Yes! And through saying yes to contributing to this book, my confidence has been further embodied.

Inspired action can also be as simple as instead of watching a movie after dinner tonight, you feel called to be outside, so you take the inspired action and spend your evening watching the beautiful colors of the sun setting. Or that awesome idea that just came through while taking a shower and taking inspired action by putting your ideas onto paper.

Another example is doing something when others doubt you, disagree, or don't get it, but You believe in yourself and still move forward—talk about courage and a quantum leap into confidence like never before; you write a whole new story with this one!

It's also trusting that, no matter what unfolds, you are listening to your heart and trusting it is for your highest evolution and expansion. Because not every time we take inspired action to move forward, it's rainbows and butterflies, but it's here as an experience for you to expand your consciousness and go beyond what "is."

When you take these soul-inspired forward movements, you are communicating that you are listening and that you trust. It's huge on your journey and allows your inner confidence to rise exponentially!

An experience that took trusting myself and my journey to another level through taking a big-time soul-inspired action into an entirely new chapter in my life comes to mind to share. All of which welcomed more soul/higher self-embodiment, a quantum leap into increased levels of confidence on my journey, and new levels of freedom! May it inspire you in some way too!

A Quantum Leap into Confidence

At the time, I had been working in the medical device industry for almost 15 years, representing various holistic medical devices to help facilitate healing for fractures, spinal conditions, and chronic pain.

From the inner love and confidence I was now living in from my 2016 spiritual awakening, in 2019, I opened my own distributorship with a specific company representing an incredible healing frequency technology for patients with chronic pain. I built up territories in California and hired and trained a team of heart-centered reps to grow and support the business which created a life of freedom for me on another level.

Shortly after, and with great love for my journey, I listened to a deep soul calling and moved to Oahu, Hawaii, where I would live for four magical years while running my California business remotely. Hawaii held and expanded me in ways words will never come close to adequately articulating. My soul gifts awakened. I listened to the inner calling to be of service to the community, and held gatherings, events, workshops, and retreats to help support others on their own spiritual awakening journeys—all of which were pathways for my confidence in my connection to source to blossom even more.

The distributorship ran on its own and was financially supporting me which was a blessing. However, even with all the success and freedom, there were intense—and at times very heavy—energetics with the company and the medical device industry that were not in alignment, and the fulfillment in the work wasn't there like it was before. But for me to walk away from that flow of income would require heaps of inner trust and greater embodied confidence.

Then I received an out-of-the-blue call from the newly hired Vice President. The company was focusing on big-time expansion and building massive revenue. He provided me with two options: grow the business or end our contract.

"Oh, wow. The time was here."

Yet, I was at a major crossroads.

My mind was saying, "Of course, it's a no-brainer, just go back into that world. Ok, so yeah it may not feel in alignment, but it's awesome money. You're good at it." I could feel myself shrinking and contracting. There was zero excitement. My heart was not in it at all anymore.

It was an outgrown version of Emily as if I was trying to fit into a pair of shoes I wore when I was a child. If I went back full-time into the medical device industry, I would be choosing the former paradigm version of Emily I had outgrown and ultimately would deny love for myself.

Limiting beliefs around money was an inner fear I would no longer defend. I chose to rise above the fear which dissolved quickly and surprised me in the most exciting ways as it spoke volumes to how far I had come.

When we rise above fear and instead listen to our heart, even when it doesn't make logical sense to the mind, we are living in full trust of self, and this is one of the most powerful ways we embody self-worth and our confidence naturally thrives!

It was a huge leap for me to walk away from a financially cushy career yet one that was no longer aligned with me. Great inner courage was activated within. I chose Love for my Soul journey into greater potential to unfold, for living life aligned with my dreams, and for stepping into even greater confidence in myself.

From my clear decision, the magic began unfolding. I had no idea if the company would keep my team of reps who were making good money and had families to support. I was calling in the highest good for everyone involved. I trusted and a miracle showed up. The company unexpectedly decided to bring on my reps as their distributors doubling their income. I didn't know that was even a possibility or viable option! Conversations with the VP had completely upleveled, everything shifted and it was unlike anything I had experienced before.

A 15-year chapter had reached its completion in my life as I headed into a new chapter and a new level of confidence and freedom had been unlocked within!

Just a few days after everything had been completed with the company, divine soul expressions of myself in higher-dimensional realms awoke even more. I spontaneously began channeling a highly evolved collective of Ascended Master Beings, and light language, a channeled form of sound energy communication, was pouring through me. I connected with soul family I had been calling in for years! Ideas, collaborations, co-creations, and inspirations were flowing in left and right. I was living in more magic and freedom than I knew was possible in the human experience. A higher state of consciousness was being embodied through allowing these new doors to be opened fully within, and I was being shown more deeply what is possible when we make choices from absolute self-love and trust in the flow of the magic of life.

It was a complete vibrational upleveling that I had summoned into my reality, which included higher levels of confidence because I was ready and said, "Yes!"

At times, it's through the choice to move beyond the fear that holds us back and letting go of the "outgrown" versions of ourselves to allow an inner rise of confidence to anchor in like never before. And I know how much courage this requires. I see you! But it's at these crossroads where you are being asked to rise and step into the "new," because You are ready and deep within, you know.

From taking the inspired action towards our soul callings and dreams, a whole new up-leveling in our consciousness and inner dimensional reality can present itself, allowing for us to experience more parts of our true essence including our naturally born confidence!

A Practice to Consider

The inner nudges, or the things that are calling us forward or exciting us, can be recognized as communication from our higher self/the Universe/Spirit helping to guide us. And through listening to this communication and making forward movements, small or large, in that direction, you are also communicating back that you trust. This is where so much magic unfolds!

Yes, sometimes it requires incredible strength and courage, but again we didn't come here to half-live life. We came here to live as the incredible souls on Earth that we are! And as you practice this more and more, it becomes easier in your day-to-day as you build the inner confidence "muscle."

An exercise that may help to build the inspired action into self-confidence "muscle" in your own life more, is to do something—say today, tomorrow, this upcoming week or month—that your heart, inner excitement, or inner knowing is calling you forward. Perhaps something bigger is calling you, but the suggestion here is to start small and keep building.

For example, maybe there's a dance class you've been super interested in taking but you've held yourself back and now choose to sign up and go! This embodies a behavior of self-trust, love for self, and inner confidence. I encourage you to honor the experience however it unfolds because this allows for even greater possibilities to flow!

In the very vibration we live from, in our choices, in our behaviors, in our actions, we are either choosing love for self or we are denying it. And when we keep choosing to live from a place of loving and trusting in ourselves, we are embodying our self-worth and inner confidence which radiates out from this powerful inner vibration.

Building self-confidence is truly your own story of coming home to you, to your absolute birthright of self-worth for incarnating on Earth at this time, of trusting yourself and knowing above all else that You are the ultimate prize and have been all along!

May this chapter be a reminder to listen to your heart, to keep choosing you, behaviors, and actions aligned with believing in yourself and loving yourself. And you will inevitably witness your confidence rising and the magic of life unfolding for you.

As this chapter arrived in its completion, a short channeled message came through from The Ascended Masters/The Higher Realms to be shared. May it uplift and inspire you on your journey!

A Channeled Message: The Gateway to Your Inner Confidence

"Blessings Dear One,

We are so grateful to connect with you in this now moment and we come to you with a vibrational message of great love and remembrance.

You are pure love come into physical form… to express yourself, your soul, and your higher self in all its fullness, completeness, and absolute knowing of the truth of who you are.

We know at times it can be perceivably challenging to remember the truth of who you are, but rest assured all of the support is here on your journey to help you remember, just as this now vibrational moment and the stories shared in this book have shown up to support you.

To be in absolute love for self is to know oneself because pure love is who you are. This knowing is deep within your being and is always available for you and your soul is continuously bringing experiences into your reality to help you remember this inner knowing.

The confidence you seek within yourself is truly the love, the absolute love for yourself. This includes trusting yourself, appreciating yourself, believing in yourself, celebrating yourself, and honoring yourself.

So yes, dear one, loving yourself is the ultimate gateway to the confidence within. And the more you choose love for yourself and the more you can witness this love that you are, the more effortless your self-confidence, appreciation, and belief in yourself will be available within you.

We celebrate your journey in all its unfolding. Our great love and support for you is always here. And with the greatest amount of love, we ask, how are you choosing to love and celebrate your self today?"

~ *The Ascended Masters/The Higher Realms* (channeled by Emily Moon)

"To establish true self-confidence, we must concentrate on our successes and forget about the failures and the negatives in our lives."

~ Denis Whitley

CHAPTER FOUR

Our Choice, Our Path: Building the Confidence Within

By Emeryelle Moore

W hat is confidence, and why does it matter? The pure definition can give us insight into its importance. The Oxford English Dictionary defines confidence as "the feeling or belief that one can rely on someone or something; firm trust." Another variation is "the state of feeling certain about the truth of something." And my personal favorite: "a feeling of self-assurance arising from one's appreciation of one's own abilities or qualities."

Why is confidence a topic we should look more deeply into, and how could it possibly have an effect on us outside of our mere interest in the meaning of a word? It would seem that this particular topic concerns the basis of trust we have in ourselves and others, and we can easily see how this would shape our entire world and how we interact with it. How it would shape who we are and what we believe. And isn't everything based on belief at a core level?

We have miracle testimonies of people who've accomplished unimaginable feats simply based on their belief that they could. I'm happy to share that I'm one of these people. Hi, I'm Emeryelle. This chapter is very close to my heart, and I'm grateful to be invited to share it with you.

I originally began building confidence by having open conversations with myself. I was honest and truthful with myself about what was happening, what I wanted, and what I didn't want. I then allowed myself to surrender to the changes that needed to happen for me to shift, transform, elevate, and completely re-begin. Was the process difficult? Of course—but only because I didn't know how to go about it. I took a deep dive into the deep end, as usual. Once I started to recognize that my enhancement, elevation, and evolution could be simple, easy, peaceful, and to my enjoyment, I began to verbally ask the Universe for things to be this way. Sure enough, things started to shift, and I allowed it.

I often use a mirror to speak with myself, giving myself all the support, encouragement, praise, gratitude, appreciation, honor, and love that I didn't feel like I had received anywhere else. After building what I would view as a healthy relationship with myself in the mirror, I began to change, and the world around me changed too. People began responding to me similarly to how I treated myself, and I began to understand that they always had. I realized what healthy boundaries look like for myself, and that I didn't need to force them or demand them. I simply became them. This is when the importance of integration, embodiment, character, and integrity came into play at a foundational level of understanding for me.

No matter where you are or who is in the room, the Universe in total responds to who you truly are at a core level and how you treat all things, including yourself. The experience and outcomes you acquire in life are determined by your focus, true desires, and affiliations, as well as how willing you are to release, cleanse, heal, and open yourself up to be transformed. To evolve. This includes what you do and who you are when "no one is looking." We are vibrational at our core, and the Universe responds in helping us hone our own unique vibration by sending us multiple frequencies to choose from. It's like a buffet of experiences: What we choose to eat at that buffet, and add to our plate each time, is what we are made of. Over time, we absolutely can completely restructure who we are, who we thought we were, and who we will become. I am happy to be a prime example that you can go from poverty, lack, addiction, disease, and pain to thriving, love, purity, abundance, magnetic, and confidence in knowing that you get to be exactly who you want to be. The question is, what does the version you want to be look like? This is where we begin.

Here are five steps that I've learned to love. They have helped me become the version that I am today, more deeply understand all the other versions that I've been, and create a process that helps get me to the next versions that are eagerly awaiting my arrival. If you choose to invite this perspective into your way of living, the versions of yourself that are eagerly awaiting your arrival will become reality too.

1. Direction—There are many important factors to consider in our journey of evolution. Direction is one of them. "Where exactly are you going?" This question sets the stage for everything that follows.

   Many times I have left the house without direction and still ended up okay. I made it. And, to be fruitfully honest, I have had a lot of fun, plenty of times. But if we have a goal, a dream, a hope, a vision, or a version of self we want to become, that's a direction.

Think back for a moment to how many times you've been able to go in more than one direction at once. If it's anything like the visual I'm seeing, I end up in something more like a spinning whirlpool, chasing my tail, still undecided on where I'm actually going. When we can faithfully choose a direction and move with it, we help to build a trait that can not only last for a lifetime but creates a solid foundation for every step we take thereafter. Confidence.

When we know where we're going, we are less likely to be taken off of the path to get there. We all know how life goes. You think you're doing one thing, and the Universe— or whatever else we like to call it—laughs. But the beauty of this is that even if the path unfolds in a million different ways, we can still arrive at the goal we set (or received from our higher versions) if we stick with the direction that gets us there. This leads to the next imperative step in building confidence, and that is...

2. Commitment—I have struggled with this term many times. "To commit or not to commit"; it's an interesting question. Why on earth would we ever not want to commit to something? What is at the base of our non-committal tendencies, and why is it a struggle for so many of us?

I can share my own understanding of it here: I believe the reason is fear. We fear that we'll make the wrong choice and get ourselves in trouble. We fear that someone will judge us for what we choose to do or who we choose to be. We fear that we will get so far in that we won't be able to turn around. I love being proof that all of that fear is nonsense, and so is the fear that drives it.

"What is the opposite of fear?" you may ask. Well, my dear, it's confidence. You are powerful, capable, strong, and worthy. You have a duty to yourself to commit to what you want and to build the confidence to do so.

It's much simpler than we think, and we are far more capable than we often give ourselves credit for. No one else can do it for you—and why would you want them to anyway? Life gets to be enjoyable when we decide how we live it. Moreover, I stand here with the confidence to say, "It will be worth every moment once you get there." But how do we overcome the fear of anything at all? Well, we face it of course. Fear is intangible and is only as big as we make it, just like anything else.

The most advantageous tool we have in building confidence is learning who we are. Once we get to know ourselves, we begin to like ourselves. We begin to understand who we are and why, how we got here, and what we're made of. We lean into trusting our own decisions when we realize how much of a difference we can make in our own lives by being intentional. And how do we cultivate that internal relationship that everything else is built from?

3. Excavation—A major component of building confidence is first learning and then deeply knowing who you are, as well as who you are not. This happens through the revealing of our levels and layers. The beauty of this process is that we

can always dive more deeply, no matter how well we think we know ourselves. Excavation into the self is a potent and powerful way to do that. By removing the layers of who other people want us to be and who we always thought we were—within the fields of conditioning, family dynamics, generational patterning, fears, undiscovered talents and desires, and by self-reflection into untended wounding and personality traits we picked up along the way—we can find who we truly want to be here.

Within each layer of self is a new version. The versions that got us through what we went through and helped us hang in there while things were tough are a necessary aspect of survival of the self, but the same toolkit you use to sand a piece of furniture won't help you fix your swimming pool. It's time for a change. That change requires a deeper look into what tools you're still using to power through life and what tools you're ready to take hold of to make life easier. Yes, such tools exist, no matter what level you're on.

We rarely know what is available to us until we intentionally ask for assistance. We also often overlook the greatest asset we have, which is being a Leader, Best Friend, and First-Hand Support to ourselves. We are an important teammate to have on our own side and imagine how much can be accomplished when we work with ourselves instead of against. We can look into the layers of who we've been and, each time, find something new about ourselves. We can discover why we did something based on who we were at the moment, what that decision led to, how we have grown over the years, and what caused our growth in each version.

We can examine the tools of life that we are using and allow ourselves the quiet audacity to learn something new about who we are here, understanding that we too are always evolving and that there is always something deeper within to be explored. Much like when we watch a movie to see something new each time, we can view ourselves in the same manner. This is why excavation is an important avenue to implement in building self-confidence.

We often don't even know what is hiding within our own layers. We may, at times, rediscover a hidden dream or unveil a hidden fear that had been driving us in a certain direction that we may not have been consciously aware of. We can repeat this five-step process indefinitely to reexamine ourselves at each new level and layer. The deeper we explore ourselves, the higher we naturally go, causing us to expand further than we may have ever thought we could.

So many times in life have I thought one thing and then done a layer of excavation and revealing work only to find that my thought was based on someone else's perspective and not my own. It was based on something someone else wanted for me, or how someone else viewed the world.

Through my willingness to explore the deeper layers of self, I found things that I never knew previous to doing this kind of self-evaluation. I found that I actually do love life and am capable of much more than some people give themselves the space for, because that's all it is. What do we have space for, and are we willing to expand for more? Do we allow ourselves room to grow, to explore, and to unlearn? How fixed are we in a mindset that could use improvement, or in a friend group that could use some adjustment? Are the thoughts we are thinking really ours? Or are they remnants of an outdated mindset or something someone told us long ago that keeps us small and unable?

We are phenomenal beings, to say the least, and self-excavation is where we find that out. So, even if it is one minute per day, no matter how advanced you think you are, allow yourself to look a little deeper into your own reflection and ask yourself, "Who am I, and why?" You may be surprised by your own answers, presenting a stronger foundation for your expanded confidence.

4. Self-Awareness—Part of this focus area concerns stepping forward enough to know that you are not the only one that experiences yourself. Every single being that you encounter experiences you as well. How are you showing up in the world? Is this question one you consider regularly? Do you have trustworthy council to offer unbiased advice, guidance, and reflection? The more you allow yourself to be seen is a direct reflection of how much you are willing to see yourself first. How can you expect to build confidence without this aspect? This question is a testament in itself to the importance of self-awareness.

The ability to increase our level of confidence has many factors, as expressed in the following questions: Where are we hiding? And how much of ourselves are we allowing to be seen, to shine, to be viewed by another person who may have an area of improvement for us to explore?

Having a council of trustworthy people is imperative to our sense of confidence. Have you ever tried carrying the world alone? How tired did doing this make you, and how far did you actually get? How much do you let yourself be supported, and how deeply do you allow another to know you? Be honest with yourself: is there room for an easier way or faster method? Look at how far you've come to this point. How much further could you reach with a network of support? For myself, the answer is simple: "Much, much further."

I used to be the version that takes everything on and beckons for "more please, Sir," because I thought the world was mine to conquer alone. It's not. There are eight billion people on this planet. I can assure you that there are many who want you to succeed, who want to help and would love to see you become who you truly want to be here.

People who are devoted to improving themselves operate from a mindset that naturally wants improvement for others, even if they aren't the ones providing it to them. This mindset is birthed when we gift ourselves the steps to build confidence. Confidence offers us the knowing that no matter what, we do have support if we want it. All we have to do is ask.

5. Self-Evaluation—Let's take a moment here. Take one deep breath in, and let it rest in your lungs for just one moment.

How does it feel? How do You feel? Are you tired?
Excited? Do you have dreams that are calling you after
reading this passage, inviting a new perspective in? What
are those dreams, and what is your plan of action to achieve
them? Do you have a new path to look into and new ways
of doing what you were doing before? When we know
where we are going and why, we get there. This is the
beauty of the process listed out here.

One focus area leads to the next, as well as back around for
us to see what we didn't, or couldn't, see before. There are
some key factors in the area of self-evaluation to look at;
they are simple and effective yet took me decades to
understand the importance of. We are the only enemy we
have, if we look at life this way; we are our greatest ally, if
we can see it this way too. The world reflects back to us
what we are, how we see things, and the way we show up,
even when we are alone in our rooms with "no one
watching."

The importance of self-evaluation necessitates that we
continue asking ourselves, "Who am I, and why?" "Where
am I going and how can I get there?" and "What is the
reason I want to go in the first place?" Our answers can give
us a deeper look at what we're doing here, and the more we
know the answer to this, the more confidently we can
approach life and everything that life offers us.

The key is always to turn the attention back onto ourselves. When
we realize that we are the deciding factor of what our core
foundation is made of, resulting in all the things that happen in our

lives, we begin to realize that no one outside of ourselves has the power to change who we are fundamentally. But, we do. People could argue that who we are fundamentally is just who we are and that's that. But "what if?" What if you learned how to choose the direction you were going in and commit to it? What if you learned how to excavate and dig deep into those core aspects of yourself that only you can? What if you learned the potency of self-awareness and self-evaluation? If you see it, you can do something about it. This means you have a grand opportunity to rebuild the core foundation of who you are and move forward with renewed confidence.

We have that power. We have that possibility. We have that potential. We have the ability to build who we are, tweak it, adjust it, amplify it, and, at unimaginable levels, completely restructure our experience based on what we choose to immerse ourselves in. The results determine how deeply we are willing to meet ourselves in those tender and vulnerable areas that only we can unlock through willingness.

When we remember that we hold the reins, it then becomes our responsibility to take care of our footprint in the world. Sure, it can be scary, but that's what our trustworthy council is for. Once we are conscious of the responsibility we have to ourselves and the way we show up in the world, everything becomes a choice. This includes how well we know ourselves, and how well we know ourselves directly results in how confident we are in ourselves.

When you know you are the driving force behind the wheel of all the experiences you have here, the rest of the world becomes a little less intimidating and a lot more fun and intriguing to explore.

Luckily, after all that excavation and relationship-building with yourself, you'll have the confidence to go out there and actually be who you came here to be: a mosaic masterpiece full of all the unique parts that, in themselves, are also a work of art to begin with. You, my beautiful, magnificent, and—now, hopefully—much more confident reader, are Art. I can only hope this passage has inspired within you the confidence to explore the masterpiece that is you and maybe even share your internal canvas with the world. We would love to meet you in your fullest expression. Now you have a new set of tools to help you get there.

"The most beautiful thing you can wear is confidence."

~ Blake Lively

CHAPTER FIVE

<hr />

Building Self-Confidence:
Uncovering the Power of Thought

By John Kelly

T he harbor wall didn't look high enough for a successful suicide attempt. But the sea was rough enough to potentially cause damage. I just didn't have the confidence that if I jumped in there, it would do the job.

Could you think of anything more embarrassing than me jumping in to kill myself? Firstly, failing, and secondly, putting people through the bother of getting me out as I bobbed about in the water, underneath the harbor wall. I could have gone up to the cliff top, but that was a four-mile walk. I had just nipped into the village to buy milk and bread for my fourteen-year-old son, who was waiting in the holiday home.

Whenever I look back at not having the confidence to even kill myself when I wanted to kill myself, I wonder: how low had I sunk? How deep had I gone into my depression without thinking there was anything wrong with it? Without thinking, "This isn't right!" Thankfully, I came out the other end.

This is my story of how I moved from that low point of confidence and self-esteem to a feeling that I describe now as being bulletproof to the "slings and arrows" of life.

At the core of what I now see to be true are three fundamental principles that have become more and more noticeable to me in my life:

1. I live in my own thought-created experience of the circumstances of my life in every moment.

2. My consciousness, or awareness, of the thought creating my reality can rise or fall.

3. At some deeper level than my thoughts and my awareness of them, I am connected to a universal energy or wisdom that guides me.

It was the noticing of these principles at work in my life that was a game changer for me in the building of my self-confidence from that suicidal low.

Crash, Understanding, Rebuilding

Until my encounter with anxiety, depression, and suicidal thoughts, I would have described my life as a model of typical steadfastness, good progression, and the epitome of the ingredients for happiness. I came from a loving family, with caring parents who lived into their nineties. I was (and still am) happily married with four brilliant children. I had progressed well academically and achieved promotion in my work from a sales representative role to becoming sales and marketing director of a nationally known and respected company.

While I would never have described myself as super-confident, especially around members of the opposite sex, I was still considered high-achieving, capable, and grounded. Yes, I had inherited what I described as my family "worry gene." Yes, this sense of worry was responsible for many sleepless nights and the occasional feeling that the pressures of the world were on my shoulders, especially if I was not hitting sales targets. But that didn't stop me from progressing. "My stress is all normal and comes with being successful," I told myself. As I approached my early forties, my self-confidence was so strong that I walked away from my corporate position, from a great paying job with a solid pension, benefits, and share options worth potentially one million euros. Instead, I became self-employed in my sales training consultancy business. Unknown to me, the leaking of my self-confidence started soon after we launched.

The first few years of establishing the business were stressful, but not unduly so in my eyes. Learning to balance the elements of being a self-employed consultant who was securing new clients, delivering the work, and running a business was stressful but doable, so long as I had an outlet for the stress through exercise. It was after exercising became difficult due to a severe leg muscle injury that the cracks in my confidence began to show. Soon, they turned from cracks to a full dam burst.

Driving to work in Dublin in late September 2005, I experienced what I thought was a heart attack. It started with a feeling that I can only describe as flatulence in my brain—a sudden burst of fullness in my head accompanied by chest pain, pain in my left arm, and pins and needles driving into my left hand. Having monitored what heart attack symptoms felt like as part of my worry gene make-up, I was confident that calling the emergency services was the thing to do.

I calmly waited by the side of the motorway, coughing to keep my heart pumping. I'd read on the internet somewhere that this had a type of massaging effect on the heart and kept it going. Have you ever noticed that not everything you find on the internet is true? The first emergency services to arrive on the scene was a passing fire tender, which I flagged down. They administered some oxygen, and their presence reassured me that at least I wouldn't die alone at the side of the motorway. The thought that struck me hard was that my faith had taught me that death is not the end; death is only the birth of eternal life.

During the moments of being perfectly well and not thinking I was dying, I could imagine myself facing death bravely and welcoming the chance to meet God face-to-face at last. But when I faced the chance of dying—or so I thought—I wasn't nearly as brave. It didn't seem like a good idea anymore; it didn't seem like the birth into eternal life. It just seemed like a premature end to an unfinished story, to a life with so much left to do, especially around rearing my family.

My trip into Beaumont hospital in Dublin was uneventful, except when the ambulance drivers asked me to explain what had happened and to list my symptoms. They had many monitors on me. They didn't need me to tell them how I felt. What I remember is that every time I relayed my symptoms to them and how the events unfolded, the heart attack symptoms reappeared. In the emergency department, I was given a taste of Dublin humour when the driver asked me to get off his trolley because they had to go back out to another call. I moaned, "I'm having a heart attack," to which the ambulance person responded, "Yes, your heart's bothering you, not your legs—now give me my trolley back."

Trolley duly returned. I was put into a wheelchair and interrogated by a junior doctor. Once again, the more I spoke about my symptoms, the worse they became again. It was a pattern I didn't recognise until much later. Even when given the chance to phone my wife, all I could tell her was, "Get my brother-in-law to collect my car from the Balbriggan Garda station, I'm having a heart attack and I'm in Beaumont Hospital . . . " and then I promptly hung up because the symptoms were returning. I didn't want my wife to hear me dying while I was on the phone with her! Thoughtful and heartless at the same time.

The upshot of my three-day stay in Beaumont hospital was a clean bill of physical health, certainly regarding my heart and any potential stomach or chest issues. "Whatever happened to you, it wasn't your heart," said the consultant who was discharging me. When I asked what it was if not my heart, he pointed to my head and said, "Have a look up here."

I didn't know it at the time, but I had just received a crash course in the Power of Thought and how it can cause overwhelming feelings within the body.

Even with this clean physical bill of health, life did not return to normal. I remember that the following week, I had a home visit from my doctor, who was so reassured by my medical report that he had no concerns for me. Despite being well physically, I was so disabled by anxiety that I could not walk upstairs to my bedroom but had to crawl on my hands and knees. From this very low point, my journey to rebuilding my self-confidence had begun.

Understanding: Uncovering the Truth of What I Am

How do you move from wanting to kill yourself and not having the confidence to carry it out, to speaking at events and conferences in front of hundreds of people? How do you develop the confidence to run a business, to meet complete strangers and talk with them about their perceived issues and their self-worth? What worked for me was that I knew I had to do something. Living a life filled with anxiety and lacking in confidence wasn't doing any good, so I looked for help. My doctor directed me to Cognitive Behavioural Therapy (CBT). This form of behavioral treatment gave me insight into my thoughts. It gave me insights into how I might try to reframe my thoughts and not make a catastrophe by turning every anxious thought into an even more anxious thought.

CBT worked for a while; I thought I was on to something, trying to move from negative thoughts to positive thoughts to reframing my thoughts. With hindsight, I can see the progress was a bit like being in a leaky boat, but I had been given a better tool with which to bail out the water. A shiny new bucket that allowed me to empty the water out of the boat quickly. The boat was still leaking, but I wasn't sinking anymore. What CBT did for me was point me toward my thoughts, the nature of thought, and my relationship with thought as the causes of my anxious feelings and lack of self-confidence. Later, a coach pointed me to the fact that "it was all thought." That my circumstances were one thing, but my experience of those circumstances was an entirely different thing, and that my experience was always linked to thought.

This was a strange concept initially. But my coach encouraged me to stay in the conversation and notice more and more the nature of thought in creating my experience and feelings about my circumstances. I was urged to notice when my experience of circumstances was different, even if circumstances hadn't changed. For example, a family member could say something that one day might have annoyed me and caused me to flare up in anger, and then another day say the same thing, with my reaction and experience being different. Increasing my awareness or consciousness around my experience of life, and the part that thought played in my experience, became a game changer for me. I began to see that my anxiety was always thought-induced.

When the cardiologist advised me to look at my head, he wasn't looking at some mental issue; he was just pointing to my relationship with thought. I received coaching and help from other people who had seen this before me. I became conscious of the fact that thought was creating my experience of life. Initially, realizing this was such a wonderful relief that I was on a high for weeks, but the high subsided. Gradually, I stopped noticing the impact of my thoughts. My worry and lack of confidence and anxiety came back, but never as badly as before. They would return if I retold my "heart attack" story, but again, that was just thought.

Invisible Rules/Embedded Thoughts

In and of itself, thought is neither good nor bad (see Hamlet). But the invisible rules, which are themselves just thoughts that have been embedded within us from infancy to adulthood, are what make us attach moral judgement on our thoughts as either good or bad. Invisible rules are the ones by which I lived my life. "Rules" such as these dictate that good behavior (as perceived by others) will be rewarded; I know my invisible rules came from my loving parents, from my church that tried to steer me right, from society, and from education. They are rules that those who exercise power over us hope will keep us on the straight and narrow.

We create the rules, even the laws of the land, often with the best intentions. The givers of the rules I adopted were mostly well-intentioned, but unconsciously, they delivered many unintended consequences. In my case, one of those unintended consequences was a case of serious anxiety and low self-confidence. My CBT counsellor summed up my issues as coming from the thought that "you are not as perfect as God and that bothers you." Rules are useful in the early stages of life, but in later life, my invisible rules or embedded thoughts became less useful as a guide for living a life of authenticity as who and what I really wanted to be.

I got to see these invisible rules as the thoughts that others had about how I should live my life. Unconsciously, I was still allowing people to hold over me the "shoulds" that I had inherited through my thinking about how to get on in life, how to please others, and how to not annoy the neighbours. Their beliefs and their thoughts had become a part of my fabric in ways I hadn't even noticed.

Rebuilding: Experiencing the Brilliant Nature of Being Human

So, what builds self-confidence? Here are several steps that can help you build self-confidence:

- Trying stuff out and seeing that the worst you thought might happen doesn't happen often.

- Trying stuff out and seeing that it works.

- Trying stuff out and seeing that while it doesn't work, you are still alright.

- Taking small steps.

- Doing something different every day.

- Talking to people who will assist, guide, and mentor.

All these steps are useful, but what was useful for me—what turned the tide for my confidence—was seeing the truth for myself of the nature of thought. Feeling the truth for myself of my connection to ultimate reality, the wisdom of the universe. Yes, I did a lot of study and a lot of reading and a lot of work on figuring out who I am, but that was my path.

Whatever path you choose will ultimately lead to the recognition that underneath thought, there is something much kinder and filled with self-compassion. There was some innate form of wisdom that was mine to access when I wasn't "up in my head" with my thinking. So, underneath this consciousness or awareness that I had about thought, I could feel something else: a quiet, inner peace. From experience and reading, my understanding grew. I could feel the confidence that comes from seeing, feeling, or knowing my connection to ultimate reality.

I understood my connection to the universal energy of life, which brought a sense of peace or what I describe as an "alright-ness." I could feel this even if I couldn't see through my thought. Even if I experienced difficult circumstances and my thoughts were turning into even more difficult circumstances, I was still alright.

The beauty of the design of being human is that, for me, those thoughts generated feelings that were uncomfortable. This warned me that my thinking was throwing me off from my inner wisdom. I could glimpse that inner confidence, the peace that many sacred books refer to as the "peace that the world cannot give." Underneath or behind what we think we are or what we are thinking, we are pure love, pure wisdom, and pure compassion.

Gradually, I understood more and more about my experiences, and within a short while, my feelings of anxiety became absent for longer and longer periods. I was slowly uncovering my innate self-confidence.

What I Now Know:

1. What's normal may not be natural.

2. Never be afraid to ask for help.

3. You can trust your inner wisdom more than your intellect. You can trust your feelings to let you know when something is off with your relationship to thought.

4. Building real self-confidence is a more an unlearning process, particularly in the second half of life.

5. Building self-esteem, a positive image of self, is a useful foundation to build self-confidence on and is a necessary part of the formative years of life.

The path for anyone trying to build self-confidence contains some foundational stepping stones. While many of these stepping stones can appear to be building self-confidence, in my experience, they are more about uncovering the self-confidence that is always present within. That self-confidence had been buried under a mountain of rubble and rubbish from my head, sometimes of my making but mostly from the thinking and the "shoulds" of others. For me and for others, I have engaged with the foundational stepping stones by taking simple actions such as the following:

- Talking with others.

- Doing something that makes you feel good and doing it regularly.

- Taking time out for yourself.

- Being compassionate and loving and nonjudgemental to yourself, and then to others.

When you notice yourself doing something that appears to erode your confidence, don't beat yourself up. Just say, "There I go again doing that thing I want to stop... isn't that interesting." This was such a powerfully helpful practice for me compared to what I used to say, which included statements like, "There I go again doing that thing I want to stop," "I'm an idiot," "I'll be no better," or "I'm just the same as my father; he couldn't change."

Whenever these stepping stones or practices take you so far, go farther by waiting for the quiet mind, noticing those times that we all can experience when our thinking quiets for us all by itself. Find activities that are conducive for you to move into the quiet space or non-thought filled mind. For me, it was when I was playing golf, focusing on just one thing—hitting the golf ball. Another activity for me was cold-water swimming; the sheer exhilaration of the feeling of being alive and energised by the cold water stopped any over-thinking and allowed me to experience my body, free from any worrisome thinking.

All these practices are useful in building self-confidence, but most helpful above all is developing an understanding of, and having an experience of, the three fundamental principles at work in all humans:

1. Noticing the thought.

2. Increasing your awareness or level of consciousness more and more about thought.

3. Experiencing the kindness of the Universal Energy of life at work in your life.

So, building self-confidence is more about uncovering the action of these principles in your life. It's about uncovering the unconscious or invisible rules, long-held thoughts that have turned into beliefs. It's about uncovering the unconscious thoughts that no longer serve your higher need and are preventing you from accessing your inner wisdom, your inner connection to the universal energy of life.

The key to my freedom from fear and lack of self-confidence has been the act of opening my level of consciousness to experience the brilliant wisdom, love, compassion, creativity, or whatever I need at the moment that will serve me well in my life. That thought-created reality seems to project for us. We are never lacking in self-confidence, but we often think we are lacking in self-confidence, which creates the feeling of no self-confidence.

See the nature of thought that makes you forget about your Divine connection. Notice that when you try stuff out and you don't have a lot riding on it (because you know you are alright), miracles can happen.

So, what are my five guiding lights in the uncovering of inner confidence, resilience, love, and self-compassion?

1. Notice the nature of thought for yourself.

2. See that your circumstances and experience of those circumstances are two different things. Your experience of the circumstances is always a product of your thinking about the circumstances.

3. Find the place of the quiet mind wherever or however that happens for you. Know that this place exists, and experience it for yourself.

4. Know that the place of peace and calm and love is always there; it never goes away even if we think it has gone away. It is still there, within us.

5. The universal energy of life is our real-time, responsive wisdom that will work for us when we need it.

The books and the literature are also wise when they tell us not to forget good food, good rest, good exercise, and good company. These are all things that can make us better within ourselves and can build self-confidence. But the greatest step in building self-confidence is uncovering the brilliant nature of our design: the love, the wisdom, the creativity, the resilience, and the confidence that rest beneath the nature of thought.

"Confidence is the ability to feel beautiful, without needing someone to tell you."

~ Mandy Hale

CHAPTER SIX

---⟶◦◦⟶---

Building Self-Trust: The Heart of Self-Confidence

By Kristen Dolan

T he word confidence originates from the Latin words con (with) and fidere (trust). Con, as a prefix, means "completely" and the verb, fidere, means "to trust." So, self-confidence would be "complete trust in oneself."

What an overwhelming concept to strive for, to have complete trust in oneself. I struggle with choosing which pants to put on in the morning to go walk the dog. As much as I'd love to stay in my comfy pajama pants, I'm quite aware of how many people I will be seeing on my morning walk, plus, I'm short, so most likely, my pajama pants will drag along the morning dew, which means my pants will get all wet, needing to change them when I get back inside anyway… and so on. Moments like these are the reasons I question my own qualifications to write a chapter called "Building Self-Confidence." But the beauty of the title is the word "building," meaning the project is not complete; it's still in the building phase, and it's a work in progress. This means that if I make the wrong choice in which pants to wear today, I trust I just gathered more information to make a better choice tomorrow.

I hope that the biggest takeaway from this chapter is how one builds self-confidence without allowing mistakes to be a fundamental part of the building process. Because someone could tell me over and over again which pants to wear, but the key to building trust with myself is learning that lesson through my own life experiences. And learning how to sit with myself after every experience—the good, the bad, and the ugly.

There are few better ways to build trust with yourself than to look deep at your reflection in the mirror when you are at your ugliest. You know those mornings after a night out, and you are wishing you could take back some of those moments that are coming back into your awareness. It takes a whole lot of experience to sit with yourself, and not search for external factors that you can blame your behavior on. But what tools and resources do you have when there are no external factors to blame? When it's just you and the mirror. How prepared are you for those life moments? To look deep into your own eyes and say, "I am here with you, we got this because I trust you, I love you, and together, we are going to discover who we become through this."

The Keys to Building Self-Confidence are Tools and Resources

Tools and resources are gained through four simple steps that create the four pillars needed to build a strong foundation in building self-confidence. They are humility, gratitude, responsibility, and maturity.

Every life experience has a purpose. We must believe this to be true. Life's grand purpose is for us to be complete or whole by being one with ourselves. To be complete is to be All One. To stand alone and have complete trust in yourself regardless of external or internal noise. To be able to move through life without the mind chatter, judgment, doubt, guilt, pity, resentment, blame, shame, envy and fear.

To be free from the limitations that keep you from creating the life of your dreams.

If we are willing to believe that we are all worthy of our dreams coming true, then we must also be willing to believe every life experience gives us access to the tools and resources to make it so.

The reason stories exist is to offer one another hope. My life is full of stories and they are all beautiful, but it's the ones that include my struggles, my mistakes, and my failures that offer the true gift I get to offer myself, as well as others.

The fountain effect of storytelling is not to serve the one telling the story but to offer those paying attention something in return. What greater offering is there than hope when there is suffering?

Life will never toss you into the deep end without first giving you enough experience to learn how to swim. Life is designed to work for you, not against you. But our misunderstanding of humility keeps us from fully embracing this truth. Too often, we believe humility is to punish and humiliate. In reality, however, it's the exact opposite. Humility is to truly know oneself. To know one's limitations, but also to know one's strengths, gifts, and talents and how to use them. Yes, life will humble you, but only because it doesn't want you jumping into the deep end before you are ready.

Our strengths, gifts, and talents are revealed to us over time. If we access them before we have the maturity to be responsible with them and the gratitude to appreciate them, then life will keep giving us experiences to strengthen our confidence in them.

Self-confidence is not believing your gifts, strengths, and talents make you better than other people. True self-confidence is committing to do your best with your strengths, talents, and gifts.

I think humility is the first key in the building process... because there are going to be life experiences that are going to ask us to get really real with ourselves. Several years ago, I committed to running a marathon. Do you ever find yourself surrounded by people who all seem to be doing a thing, and somehow, you're the odd one out? So, at 40 years old, I decided I would join them because I was in that phase of my personal development where I was going to affirm and empower myself that I could do anything that I set my mind to.

And yes, while that's true, we also need to humbly accept where the body is at in our goals and what the body can do. When the mind and the body are not on the same page or timeline, it can make the thing you are trying to do rather frustrating. Thinking and doing exist in two different realms, and what separates them is time.

What I failed to realize is most of these people I was comparing myself to—those running marathons at my age—had been running as a form of exercise for years and genuinely enjoyed running. So, taking up something that I had no experience with while refusing to admit to myself that I did not enjoy running meant that the time it was going to take to achieve my goal was way longer than what my mind was willing to accept. And I can tell you the running season of my life was not a pretty one.

I really wish this story had a beautiful ending with me crossing the finish line, arms raised high, feeling so proud of myself, and the unwavering self-confidence I gained from it, but that is not how it went at all. I ended almost every training feeling disappointed and discouraged with myself. It has taken many years (maturity) to see the lack of humility, gratitude, and responsibility in being honest with myself because I was forcing myself to do something that I did not like at all. I was forcing my body to do something that felt terribly unnatural to me. I was not honoring the time I truly needed to invest in my training if I wanted better results. So, if building self-confidence is about achieving trust in oneself, this experience took years (and years) to gain that trust back between my mind and my body. Because, instead of building upon it, I was damaging it.

I now understand that I forced myself into an experience that was fueled by an external source. I allowed my mind to be influenced by something external of me. When it really wasn't about running a marathon; it was about building a stronger relationship and trust in myself when faced with a challenge. And I was forcing this experience on my body and not honoring my body.

I know there are some extreme examples in this world about when something is forced upon the body, but if we want to build self-confidence, we must take responsibility for how much is forced upon our bodies each day. Consider the simple act of drinking coffee. How often do we pause long enough to check in with the body and introduce the idea of having a cup of coffee vs. just drinking it because it's a force of habit? Allowing our bodies to have a voice in how we live life is a powerful way to build trust with ourselves.

Learning to trust that every life experience is an offering to know oneself better. And each experience involves all of me: my mind, body, and soul. We are all in this together.

Why Building Self-Confidence and Trust within the Mind, Body and Soul Matters

The reason it is so important to know yourself. The reason why building self-confidence and trust within yourself is so important is because there will be a day when what you are building needs to stand alone. How strong will your foundation in your belief and trust in yourself be when that moment comes?

Imagine the process of building your self-confidence, using the image of a tower. As floors are added, we have a foundation and four pillars to hold the structure strong.

The floors are the truths you stand upon—your belief system—also known as consciousness.

For many, a collective consciousness builds our tower—a set of beliefs a collective group agrees to believe in and put their trust in. For the greater part of my life, this is what my self-confidence was built upon. I trusted the belief system of going to college, getting a job, getting married, building a house in the suburbs, having kids, driving a minivan… and so on.

And I built one hell of a tower for all to see.

I built my entire life around this tower, surrounded by towers that looked almost exactly like mine. I was confident because I felt safe in my tower… until I didn't…

I remember waking up one day, and suddenly, this tower I had lived in with such confidence no longer resonated. I felt confused and lost, as if I were suffocating within the walls of my tower.

I can use the term 'no longer resonated' now, but at the time, I had no idea what was happening. This perfect life I had built upon a belief that, if I checked all these boxes, I would be happy, was actually making me unhappy.

Instead of honoring what I was feeling, trusting this gut feeling that some changes needed to be made for myself, I did the opposite. I put my head down and tried to force myself to live in this tower because cognitive dissonance was in full force, so I lacked the maturity to see that what I was feeling was more important than the image I had created. I held on so tightly to the image, powering through each day, following the set of rules within the collective consciousness I was living in. Keeping my tower up and looking like everyone else's tower.

Until this moment happens in our life, when our allegiance to the image is stronger than our allegiance to our soul, we create upheaval for ourselves.

The foundation of the tower is rooted in the soul. The value system and the four pillars of humility, gratitude, responsibility, and maturity deeply align with the soul, not the image we align with. I was committed to my image, and life became hard. The ease with which I once flowed through life was gone. The simple things that brought me joy became scarce. Everything felt forced.

Add the "Be Grateful" movement, and now that feels forced, too. I was forcing myself to be grateful for a life that looked good to everyone else, but inside, I felt awful. I was consumed with guilt that I wasn't grateful for all the things I was told to be grateful for. The fact that I had a journal so I could write down what I was grateful for should have been the biggest red flag—shouldn't gratitude naturally flow through me? Why would I need to set time aside each day to tell myself what I was grateful for? Unbeknownst to me, there was a growing gap in my life.

My tower was full of confusion, doubt, blame, shame, judgment, and resentment. Life became so heavy, except here is the scary part... I still could not admit to myself that I wasn't happy and that something needed to change.

My four pillars were stuck because humility was non-existent. I was not being honest with myself. I wasn't feeling grateful even though I was telling myself to be grateful. I wasn't taking any responsibility for myself because all of my time and energy was spent maintaining the tower—the image I showed to the world—to keep it looking good. Because I couldn't let anyone inside, and as long as it looked good, then no one would know the truth. A truth I wasn't mature enough to admit to myself. Therefore, there was no growth, movement, or flow to me. Instead of expanding, the walls of my tower were closing in on me.

My life became stagnant, and you know what happens to stagnant water... it becomes a harbor for disease and bacteria to grow. And guess what happened... I got sick. Very, very sick. And my tower came crashing down, shattering my self-confidence.

Autoimmune disease took over my body. My joints raged with pain; the inflammation was so bad I couldn't bend any of my fingers more than 45°. I was having seizures. I had terrible brain fog; my memory was so clouded. Life became pure survival. It felt like my confidence would never return.

My commitment to the image was no longer enough to carry me through the day. The gap between my mind, my body, and my soul was huge. I was humbled to my knees. My tower built on an image could no longer be sustained because I had to become my priority. I had to learn how to build my tower from my heart center—from the inside out—to start saying yes to me without needing the acceptance of those outside of me.

I needed to build a tower that was a reflection of just me, not a tower that required the approval of others. But one that was authentically me. One without walls to keep my truth and my image separate from one another.

A great quote by Prince:" To create something from nothing is how heaven is built."

I had to build myself up and pick myself up from a very dark place. Being sick with an autoimmune disease takes its toll on the body; my mental state was traumatized. I felt like such a failure—like a fraud. I felt like I was nothing. I was so angry at myself for falling for a narrative that wasn't mine. And the icing on the cake—it's really expensive to be sick. I was consumed with stress from every area of my life. My health, my wealth, my marriage, my career, and my social life were all in my face, demanding my attention.

My life had to become so simple because moment to moment was all I could handle. I had to learn how to stand again and the beginning of the rebuilding process of self-confidence was critical. The foundation I was standing upon needed to be deeply rooted so I could rise and stand tall in a new way. I couldn't go back to what was. I had to start with me at the center and build from there.

I had to be vulnerable and honest with myself. I had to rediscover myself and know what aligned with me at my core, not my false image. I had to be real about what felt good and what didn't. I had to learn to say no to things I normally said yes to out of obligation. I had to accept that not everyone was going to like or support this new me.

Here's the funny thing about building self-confidence and trust in yourself: It's going to cause a lot of relationships in your life to shift. People you thought would be in your life forever suddenly feel like you have nothing in common with them, and even more heartbreaking, some will feel like your enemy. This happens because you are now a threat to their image—an image that bonded the two or three or more of you. And now you are causing a glitch in their circuitry.

This is when I learned how my autoimmune disease became one of my greatest gifts. It became my opportunity to share my story and my experience so that no one else had to get as sick as I did. Just by learning how to say yes to myself and no to the false image. An image based on a set of agreements to keep the status quo going.

Because who does the status quo serve?

If you are serving the status quo, you are not serving you. The status quo does not want you to be an individual. It wants you to be just like everybody else. Without self-confidence, it's really hard to go up against the status quo. That need to be just like everyone else is deeply programmed into the brain. For a long time, it was how we all survived. A herd mentality, a hive mindset, has its purpose until you outgrow it.

Moreover, with self-confidence, you will know when it's time to leave the hive. You will know, deep within you, that it's ok to leave and let go of a belief that no longer serves you. Because, with self-confidence, you have the humility to know what's serving you and what's not. You can be grateful for its purpose while you need it. You can take responsibility for the lessons learned and apply them. You are mature enough to grow out of where you were so you can become more of who you are meant to be.

If keeping the status quo was in our nature... then, well... nature would not exist as we know it. There would be no butterflies, as the caterpillar would never surrender to the faith of its next stage of life. A flower would never bloom, as the plant would never surrender into what else it could be. A seed would just remain a seed, and life would cease to exist.

The seed must be willing to deconstruct completely what it was to allow the sprout inside to come to life.

Even if the seed has the vision that it's a flower, the growth process requires space and time. It must honor where it is at, moment by moment, and not judge what it's not, but trust what it is, for it will never be able to bloom fully without honoring all the steps to get there.

It can be humbling to stand where we are, look up to where we are going, and see all the steps to get there.

But a beautiful thing happens when we are fully aligned with the foundation of who we are and the faith that life is always preparing us for what we are to become. We are gifted with clarity.

Clarity cleans away all the misunderstandings. It edits the stories that hold us back, especially the stories where the victim role became such a natural role to play. Clarity empowers us with faith, hope, grace, and joy, because clarity allows me to be where I am, without questioning why. It shifts the question from why is this happening to me, to what purpose is this serving me.

Suddenly, the building process no longer feels like a job. It is now who I am. And who I am is unfolding with each life experience before me.

I am a work in progress, full of endless possibilities to be discovered. Deeply and humbly aware that every step of the process has served its purpose. Grateful for it all. Always willing to take responsibility for the opportunities and lessons life is offering. Allowing my maturity to unfold with each life experience.

For what would be the point if we were all here to be the same? When I envision the potential of humanity, it's not black or white. It's a spectrum of colors, each with a unique frequency, harmonizing, playing, discovering, and expanding into more while deeply rooted in the confidence of themselves.

Without self-confidence, how would you ever discover how to stand tall upon the faith in the process? For I am a mind, a body, and a soul with a spirit guiding me every step of the way.

Some Key Takeaways for Building Self-Confidence

The four Practices of Humility, Gratitude, Responsibility, and Maturity give us access to all of the tools and resources we accumulated through the process of building self-trust, the heart of self-confidence:

Humility: Keeps Me Grounded in the Truth of Who I Am

What is your comfort level when sitting with yourself? Do you allow the mind chatter to be heard? Or do you try to stuff it down? How will you know what is yours vs. an outside influence without listening to your thoughts?

A great practice is to get some paper and start writing out the thoughts that come up. Allow the mind chatter to pour out of you. And then, read it. Decide what resonates and what does not. Make edits. Question the thoughts. Get curious. If the mind can be controlled by thoughts, then we must be willing to take the time to control our thoughts.

Repeat this practice daily and weed out what does not serve you. Practice grace and compassion for what comes up, as there will be parts of you that surface that you have been avoiding for a long time. True confidence is the humility to see ourselves and love ourselves fully, but the fullness of our love is rooted in the depth of how willing we are to know ourselves. Confidence is trust in what we know. Faith is trust in the unknown. The goal is to come into harmony in both the known and the unknown parts of ourselves, and humility offers us the tools to master feeling confident in the dance between both.

Gratitude: Invites My Awareness That Life is a Reflection of Who I Am

Are you able to allow life to be a true reflection of you? How do we get to know ourselves truly without a mirror reflecting back at us? Allowing life to be that mirror is not always easy, but once we accept its purpose, we can get to work on building a life that feels like a true reflection of us, not an image for someone else's approval.

The embodiment of gratitude invites us to play with life and welcomes that it will give me the tools and resources I need to become the version of myself that welcomes the opportunity to work with what is before me to help me grow and expand into more of who I am. Life is not going to give me more of what I want if I am not grateful for what I have now.

Money is a great tool to work with when learning how to be in gratitude, as money was created as the physical expression of gratitude, not to entitle me to things that are not in my true alignment. Start practicing gratitude whenever you have to pay for something… especially your bills. The more we begin to find ourselves in a state of genuine gratitude for all that we have in life, the more opportunities we will be given to receive more. You will be amazed at the confidence gained through this practice, as you will begin to see everything around you as an expression of gratitude for you.

Responsibility: Reminds Me I Am Not Separate from My Actions

What is your ability to respond to what is before you? I often use the term bandwidth when exploring responsibility, as my ability to respond is rooted in my bandwidth to handle it. Building self-confidence requires a level of responsibility; the more confident we become, the more abundant life will be, which sounds wonderful. Who doesn't want to live a more abundant life? But being more abundant means we have the bandwidth to be more patient, more forgiving, more compassionate, etc. So if I find myself being triggered, then I am choosing judgment over grace or blame over acceptance, then I am not being responsible with what is being shown to me.

And here is the key to expanding my ability to respond: let go of believing your response was wrong. Shift your mindset into believing a trigger is an invitation to bring a blind spot into view. Accept it as a gift—a trigger is life's way of showing that you are ready to step into more of who you are, and here is something that is getting in your way. As you master this exchange with life, your bandwidth will expand as you've proven to be able to respond to life from a space of love and not fear.

Maturity: The Gift of Growth & Expansion into More of Who I Am

Have you allowed the mind, body, and soul to be at the same stage of wisdom? As wisdom is only gained through personal experience. Maturity is the culmination of humility, gratitude, and responsibility for life's experiences. And when we are in daily practice with all three, we are developing our own growth cycle of trust with oneself.

We are surrounded by proof that this maturation process leads to great change and transformation. The butterfly, wine, flower, etc., all began as one state of being and grew, transformed, and matured into something beyond their original state.

This process is a balance in confidence in oneself while being in faith that I am always growing and expanding into more, for it is the self that is expanding out into more. The heart of who you are is at the core of what you are building.

So stay humble, be grateful, welcome responsibility and surrender into maturity so you can build the self-trust to allow your heart to be the source of your self-confidence.

"Be so confident in who you are that no one's opinion, rejection, or behavior can rock you."

~ Unknown

CHAPTER SEVEN

Landing on My Feet

By Joanne Mengwasser

S elf-confidence sometimes comes out of sheer necessity. In fact, I never really considered myself to be self-confident. I just knew what I wanted, or more accurately, what I didn't want. That drove me to take actions I may not have taken had my life been different. As Tony Robbins often says, "Life happens for us, not to us." For this reason, I am grateful for all the events of my life, even if I didn't fully appreciate them at the time.

I rarely had the opportunity in school to be on my own in a classroom because my older sister, Lisa, was thirteen months older than me and we went to a tiny Catholic grade school where there were two grades per room. As a middle child, one year she and I shared a room and the following year, my twin younger sisters, only nineteen months younger, and I shared a room.

During our school years, it seemed that Lisa made a point of letting everyone know how undesirable (to put it mildly) I was, so that no one actually took the time to get to know me. My first clue that something was off was in the last week of seventh grade, when the eighth graders, my sister's class, were awarded their final week of school off. After sitting around in a group discussion that included my entire class of eight students, a boy who had been a classmate for all seven years turned to me and said, "You know, you're not so bad." That week was the best week of my entire grade school experience, up to that point. For the first time in nearly seven years, I truly felt free to be me and that, as it turns out, was acceptable to my fellow seventh graders.

I don't think I quite understood the magnitude of my classmate's statement at the time, but it became much clearer as I progressed through high school. I felt the same heaviness fall over me that I couldn't quite place throughout grade school. My teachers reported to my parents that I was quiet and friendly and followed the rules, so the fact that I was an outcast didn't make sense. My self-doubt was enormous during those years. I have so much more clarity when looking back now.

Fortunately for me, my sister found a boyfriend in high school and wanted to marry him, but college had to come first. She was very book smart and graduated high school a semester early to head off to college. My freedom began that semester, along with my confidence. It was clearer than ever that she had something to do with my hardships through school, so I was determined not to follow her to college as well, and given that she had gone north to school, I chose to go south.

It didn't occur to me at the time that I was being brave by heading in a different direction than she had, although I had often been told that I was brave to go to such a large school an hour away from home. It is truly amazing what you can do when pushed to a limit. I had discovered freedom for myself with increased confidence and wanted that to continue at whatever cost.

The college that I chose was a much larger school than Lisa was attending, and I dove into all the activities. Yes, it was scary at first, but the more I got involved, the more comfortable it became, as tends to be the case with confidence. It helped that my dorm floor consisted of only about a dozen girls, and we grew close quickly. Most of us were freshmen, so we formed a bond of friendship that allowed us to explore much of college life together. There were also a couple of upperclassmen sprinkled in to help show us the ropes. Among us, there were at least a few willing participants for almost any adventure any of us might dream up. If someone heard about a party, a group of us would plan to go. If someone was interested in a guy, she could generally find at least one other person eager to back her up. When it came to studying, we often had a buddy to study with, if not a full group.

I seized any opportunity I saw to stretch myself and experience the world around me. Given an opportunity to study abroad, or rather, get three credit hours for spending thirty days in seven countries on a tour bus with a group of twenty girls, I was in! We came back with plenty of stories to tell, though we had visited more churches than anything, but Wow What a trip!

It wasn't only my sister that pushed me to be independent. I knew, even then, that if I didn't do something different, I would be stuck in that small town (population: 5,600) for the rest of my life. That was a smothering thought to me. I wanted so much more for myself than a small town offered, even if I didn't fully understand the enormity of it. To me, living in a small town meant eternally working at a minimum wage job. Although that may not have been entirely true, that was my view of the world and I wanted so much more from life than that.

I graduated college in the customary four years, only to find out that there was such a thing as a five-year plan. If only I'd known! Truthfully, though, four years was enough. I had incredible experiences and formed amazing friendships, but I was done with the classroom.

After graduation and a brief stay back home, with a gentle nudge from my mom because I had applied to a job about three hours away, I moved to St. Louis to be available should I be offered an interview. Again, this was a big step, but by moving in with my aunt, I had a bit of a gentle landing. She was there to show me around and help to ease my transition.

Confidence, to me, is moving forward even in the face of some fear. It certainly helps to have a bit of a cushion when you land, but mostly it comes from taking the leap and growing wings on the way down. The moves I had made up to this point had taught me that staying put was often scarier than taking a leap into the glorious unknown. As my mentor, Mary Morrissey, often says—and I'm paraphrasing—"Our spirit longs for a freer, fuller, and more expanded expression of itself by means of itself." I felt this feeling very early on and knew that remaining in what some would consider a comfortable life would choke me.

I have had some fabulous experiences in my life, expanding my confidence in my ability to land on my feet in the process.

I got the job that I had applied for a few weeks after moving to St. Louis. Although I spent about six and a half years on this assignment, the textile industry was still a bit stuck in the past. Their management had generally been born into the industry and they weren't sure what to do with someone who was college educated, so

I lost my job. On my way home that day, I was already looking forward and making plans for what was next. I was free from a job that had been pulling me down and I hadn't even realized how much until it was over. This change, along with the fact that my apartment lease had expired a week earlier, seemed to form a new alignment of the stars for me. Due to low funds, even prior to losing my job, I had taken on a job as a server in a local Mexican restaurant to supplement my income. After being laid off from my primary job, I was offered an opportunity to move to Tennessee to work in a steakhouse that a friend who I had been working with in the Mexican restaurant would be managing. I needed to do my due diligence and take a road trip to Tennessee to check it out, but in less than a week, I was packed and moving. Here I was landing on my feet again, and confident that nothing could keep me down for long.

Two short years in Tennessee and countless experiences later, it was time for change again. I was loving life and doing well, but the restaurant industry, at least according to my mom, did not qualify as a 'real job.' My training was in textiles and my wise uncles thought that maybe North Carolina, where most textile jobs were located, would be a good place to be. Fortunately, one of those uncles lived there, so once again, I had a soft landing. A textile job, however, never materialized, as my timing somewhat coincided with the demise of the textile industry in America.

Retraining in computers seemed to be my next best option. That started me on a sixteen-year career path with a pharmaceutical company, which ended when the outsourcing of technical jobs became the norm, just two months after losing my mom to cancer.

A string of subpar jobs followed, which clipped my confidence a little, but these jobs taught me once and for all that I was not cut out for the 'box' (in my mind, anyway) that is the corporate environment. I felt far too hemmed in and held down by the rules. I needed to break free again. Oddly, as I mentioned earlier, I never really thought of myself as self-confident. To me, I was just moving forward. Looking back, however, I rarely shrank from an opportunity, especially if it meant improving my life in some way. Change has always been more intriguing to me than staying the same. A recent conversation with a long-time friend revealed to me he had always considered me to be self-confident. It's interesting that the impression we have on others is often very different from what we believe of ourselves.

Another uncle (I have so many!) told me he enjoyed traveling with Lisa and me because we were always willing to try something new. Yes, Lisa and I had become very close in our adult years. Sadly, Lisa died at only 46 after a seemingly short battle with a brain tumor. I took my uncles' compliment as high praise because I have found that being willing to try nearly anything at least once has led me to some amazing experiences. Fear stops so many people from trying new things. I feel bad for them because we only have this one chance at life and new opportunities are the juice that we can squeeze from life to make it so much richer.

One of the many skills that I have learned in my life that has had a huge impact on my confidence is quilting. My first quilting lesson came well over forty years ago, while I worked at a department store during high school. I had been sewing most of my life because my mom was quite proficient at sewing and curiosity drove me to pick up the skill almost as if by osmosis, but certainly with mom's assistance. In fact, when I took a Home Economics class in high school and the other students had chosen a simple skirt to make, I had chosen a button-down, collared shirt and still finished weeks before anyone else, even though the skill required is far greater. I then assisted my classmates in completing their projects.

Quilting was one craft Mom had no experience at and, therefore, hadn't taught us. We had learned nearly any other craft available from her. We had also taken part in 4-H and Girl Scouts, where we learned even more. After all, my mom had four girls in the late 60s and her primary job seemed to be to raise potential wives.

My first quilting project was a hand-pieced, hand-quilted, quilt-as-you-go, queen-size quilt. This experience deepened my confidence to trust my intuition with quilting and life. I was very much a die-hard proponent of hand quilting, agreeing with the popular opinion of the time that machine quilting was not authentic. My grandma, who was part of a church group that met twice a week for a traditional quilting circle, may have influenced that opinion. However, she commented several years later, 'If they had had machines back when, they would have used machines.' This transformed my view of quilting. Since that time, I have become an avid machine quilter, even doing so for others as a business for a period. Sometimes I long for a simpler time when I took the time to hand quilt.

After moving to North Carolina in the late 90s, I got much more involved in quilting. I worked at a local quilt store and got involved in the local quilt guild and smaller quilting groups. I also taught some classes at the store. I obviously spent an abundance of my time quilting. As with anything, the more time you spend doing something, the more you learn, and the better you get at it. In fact, one of my quilting buddies once commented that I was quite prolific at it. At some point, I seemed to become the go-to person in my various groups when anyone had a question, especially with quilt math issues. I had always been good at geometry and that skill is almost a necessity with quilting.

Working efficiently was also a skill that I had honed over the years. If I could find a better and faster way to complete a task, I would certainly do so. I like to think that I learned this skill from my dad. His medium was wood (building houses) and mine was fabric (making quilts), but I am proud to have gained the base skill from him. People often commented that he worked faster than anyone they had seen and his was always quality work. My quilting friends often say that I quilt in 'Joanne time' because I do my best to do things more efficiently, being conscious at the same time to not let the quality suffer.

I am not perfect, but spending a considerable amount of time honing a skill inevitably boosts one's confidence. I have even been told by students that I am very patient when teaching quilting. This comes from the knowledge that learning anything new takes time and everyone deserves to learn at their own pace. Some will find that a new skill is not something that they want to continue, and others fall in love with a process and want to continue learning more. If someone rushes the learning process, they are much less likely to want to continue. I wanted to give them every opportunity to fall in love with it just as I had, while fully understanding that no new skill is meant for everyone.

My dad once asked me, "So, you cut fabric apart, just to sew it back together again?" Had I been thinking, I might have posed the same question back to him about building houses. (So, you cut wood apart, just to nail it back together again?) It truly is the same concept but with a different medium to work with. Even though I lost my dad over six years ago, it's comforting to think that we have both been artists in our own way. He was very skilled at building houses because he had done so for several decades. In fact, after his first business failed due to a bad partnership, he moved to a new city, started over and built quite a lucrative business on his own, all from nothing more than word-of-mouth advertising. You might even say that his starting 'safety net' was the fact that he had several brothers and brothers-in-law living in the area needing work on their houses. He also worked for many of their neighbors and friends once word got out that he was doing great work at reasonable prices.

Naturally, my parents were both significant role models for me for most of my life. They provided guidance and discipline when I needed it and let me pave my way when I could do so. I have continued to have role models and mentors throughout my life who have helped me in one way or another. Some are still present in my life today. Who we receive guidance from over our lifetime can change frequently, but having role models helps us to reach for another level in our life. They show us what can be possible for us, assisting us in growing our confidence and allowing us to achieve what we might not have otherwise considered attainable.

Being a part of a group can also help us to have accountability and provide feedback when we reach for a new level in whatever aspect of life that we choose. Many of my mentors have repeated that 'lone ranger syndrome,' or attempting to do it all on your own, will only get you so far. There are many things you can do in life alone, but often, in order to advance to a new level, it is helpful and even necessary to have coaches or mentors around to boost you up and show you what may have taken them years to figure out. Perhaps they learned it from a mentor of their own, essentially condensing decades into days, allowing you to achieve your goals much faster than it would take to reinvent the wheel, so to speak. Being open to this type of guidance can be extremely helpful, but you are also free to take from it what serves you and leave the rest behind or set it aside for a later time. You are ultimately the highest authority in determining what serves you and your path in life.

I have had more than one mentor say that proximity is power. If you are the smartest one in the room, you are in the wrong room. You should spend time with people who are smarter than you so that you stretch yourself to be better every chance you get. This is how we grow in confidence and pave our way in life.

When learning any new skill, self-doubt may inevitably creep up, but having a support system around you and setting realistic, achievable goals will help to build your confidence in that skill. Additionally, it is imperative that you celebrate even the small wins as you go. Your confidence stems from your willingness to be brave enough to leap into the unknown when a new opportunity presents itself. The more you leap, the more you discover you are not only capable but skilled at landing on your feet. Progress is so much more important than perfection.

Tony Robbins says that perfection is the lowest bar you could reach for because expecting perfection is simply how we mask the fear of taking action. Done is always better than perfect.

One thing is guaranteed: you will fail. But successful people are willing to fail enough to succeed. Thomas Edison, after 50,000 attempts at creating the light bulb, said, "I never had a failure. I had 50,000 pieces of feedback." This is how we should all be looking at our lives, especially if we have a specific goal in mind. We only fail when we quit.

"With confidence, you have won before you have started."

~ Marcus Garvey

CHAPTER EIGHT

---∽o◖✐◗o∼---

Know and Expand Thyself: Cultivating an Attitude of Latitude

By Heather Price

I s it time for you to embrace the attitude of latitude to expand your bubble of beliefs, liberating your most magnificent archetypes, opening your heart to miraculous experiences to confidently reclaim your worth?

Before we begin this journey together, let's define the word 'latitude' within the context of building self-confidence as *an expansion of thought, intention, and action beyond any limiting beliefs and old patterns we may be playing out.* The guidance here is to *think outside the square!*

It has been my experience, personally and professionally, as a long-time wellbeing counsellor, coach, mentor, practitioner, and trainer of shamanic path and practice, that a person with low self-confidence is usually unable to move forward because they are stuck in some kind of restrictive archetypal pattern carrying limiting beliefs and low vibrational patterns that diminish their self-image and esteem. For example, a strong archetypal presence of The Doubter, and perhaps the Victim, can cause indecision and depressive feelings. The Doubter could arise from being restricted by what was learned from past experiences that no longer, if ever did, serve anyone. The Victim may be trapped in the habit of taking everything, including other people's projections, personally rather than keeping strong personal and professional boundaries. Other well-known examples or archetypal influences known to cause or be caused by a lack of self-confidence are the Procrastinator, the Pessimist, and the People Pleaser. There are sure to be others that you are familiar with.

There can be other less understood influences that you may carry from beyond your experience in this life that can create a dip in self-confidence, such as imprints from primary caregivers, ancestors, and unfinished business from a past life, or you may be influenced by astrological patterns and birth sign traits. The positive thing is that once you have identified the archetypal and genetic patterns that are causing a lack of self-confidence, you can work at creating new, liberating beliefs and healthy attitudes that give latitude and license to live, love and lead in spirited, self-confident ways.

Diminished self-confidence is not always dominated by past patterns and trauma responses; it can also come about because you are facing unfamiliar experiences. You may be studying a new course or taking on a new position in your work, or perhaps facing an intimate relationship or parenthood for the first time. Or maybe you are helping a loved one move through an unexpected illness or supporting an elder in your family through their last stage of life. During these kinds of times, you may be visited by familiar archetypal voices and turn to old, limiting ways to get through the day.

Fortunately, there are other more powerful and significant truths and archetypal energies that can be uncovered within your soul's coding—if you are willing to take the time to re-evaluate significant and challenging times of confrontation and trauma through a lens of self-love and compassion, with a belief in self-healing, a new attitude, and a clear understanding of your values. Adopting this approach can immediately transform the emotional energy vibrating within your light body, which surrounds your physical body, enabling you to make new, healthy decisions and take amazing new pathways. This way of facing and transmuting limiting ways of being, through alchemic reframing, which could also be described as shamanising[1], is the way of the Luminary, Transformer, Shapeshifter, Liberator, Warrior, and Co-Creator.

Here are a few personal stories that I hope may help you understand some of the points I have made about what may impact your self-confidence in both restrictive and positive ways. It is my hope that one or more of these stories may be relatable to your pathway of discovering the riches that warm your heart.

Stories of Losing and Finding My Way to Self-Confidence

Sitting on the mailbox outside my home while rain poured heavily down over me, I allowed myself to weep and fully let go of the pain I was feeling in my heart. For eight years my youngest son had been troubled by major physical, neurological, and emotional injuries that caused him to have little or no control over his behaviour. Earlier that desperate night in the rain, I had lost control, and my temper, reaching rock bottom as a mother. Left with no answers for my son and no confidence in myself to find answers that could relieve our

---

[1] Adam Rock and Stanley Krippner (2011). Demystifying Shamans and Their World: A Multidisciplinary Study. Pub: Impact Academic.

family from the pain we had all endured, I called out to God, begging for my son's healing and offered in exchange to be in service to those in need of help and healing for the rest of my life. I was a reasonably successful professional artist and had dreams of creating a life with a new partner; however, I was willing to let it all go in exchange for my son to live a healed and peaceful life.

During this time and leading up to this deal with God, I had left my marriage and moved from the country to the city on a mission of getting help for my son and our broken family. I had read every book on raising sons and on how to support children with challenges that I could find—some I had read more than once. I joined a support group as well as seeing a psychologist for help. My doctor at the time had far more confidence in me than I did in myself, and as he watched my relentless pursuit to find an answer for my son, he helped me keep going. In one appointment I had begged him to refer my son to a psychiatrist for a diagnosis and medication and he had gently encouraged me to keep stretching beyond any limitations that arose and to continue listening to my intuition. Though I had little confidence in myself, my doctor had bucket loads of it in me!

Now, sitting out under the relentless rain in a deep place of powerlessness, shame, prayer, and surrender, I had fallen as low as I could go and felt there was nothing more I could do but to hand over the care of my son to someone who would keep him safe. My promise to lead a life of service in exchange for a cure for my son was one last, desperate plea to the Universe and God before doing so.

Recently I found myself in a similar situation where I felt helpless and afraid, desperate to find a way to help a loved one heal and to save her family from years of trauma. However, I recognised the pattern of self-sacrifice and the archetype of Saviour before getting to the point of making a plea or deal with God. Instead of rushing in and giving all I had by rescuing my loved ones from a world of pain and exhausting myself from over-giving, I have stepped confidently into the role of Mentor and taken consistent, steady steps to affirm, educate, and guide family members involved, mentoring them to step into their power and find their own way through this dark time. At least that is the plan, and I have to constantly watch myself to ensure I stay in the role of Mentor and Guide—Wise Aunty—so as not to take on the old roles of Rescuer and Saviour.

Fortunately, over time, I have come to know myself well and recognised the archetypal patterns that have led me into dark and desperate patterns in the past, causing me to lose my self-confidence and to doubt myself and mistrust my soul's journey. My patterns of self-sacrifice and fear of what others might think if I share my vulnerability and ask for help has been transformed over many years of careful observation and self-reflection. Alongside of this, I have recognised that it is not God punishing or saving me when things go wrong, rather it is my soul attempting to balance out my life and steer me onto the path where I am called and destined to be of best service. Instead of feeling powerless and afraid of what others might think of the choices I make, I have learned to stand my ground and venture pathways less travelled fearlessly and ask for affirmation and encouragement from those soul travellers I can rely on when I need it. I have journeyed long and deep over many years to get to truly know who I am and why I am here, learn to love the many aspects of myself that allow me to be uniquely me, and respect the choices I make.

That desperate, rainy night pleading with God had a very happy result at the time, however I have since learned not to make deals of any kind and to listen to and be guided by my intuition to lead me to greater, self-empowering ways to manage desperate situations. I remember waking the next morning after that dark night feeling completely drained, yet there was also a strange feeling and energy of relief moving and pulsating through me. I remember allowing that strange feeling inside of me, which I came to eventually know as my intuition and inner guidance, to guide me while standing in the kitchen and reaching out to a book by Sue Dengate on the bench with a feeling of certainty that it had a message for me. I read Sue's two books *Different Kids* and later *Fed Up*, from cover to cover several times searching for clues what I might be feeding my son that could be causing him to have such reactive behaviours. I had tested him by taking him off numerous foods containing preservatives. For some reason I had been blinded to the information that round bread contains preservatives until that day, the day after making my deal with God.

Now it stood out to me like a written siren—clear as a bell. I knew my son had passionately loved eating bread! Why hadn't the veil lifted for me to see this until now? I immediately searched for a company that made bread without preservatives and everything changed. Unbelievably, after eight years of struggling to find what was clearly affecting my son's wellbeing, there were no more challenges or tantrums. The veil of absolute pain and agony of not being able to heal my son from his troubling life had finally lifted. For me and my family, it was nothing short of a miracle.

Beautiful synchronicities followed 'the deal.' I found an advertisement in the paper announcing that someone coming to my suburb to teach Reiki, so I rang and booked in to learn this ancient craft of hands-on energy healing. Following on with my commitment, I enrolled in an advanced diploma and later a degree in counselling and as things began to fall easily into place, my self-confidence and faith in a higher power watching over me gradually began to return. At the same time, my budding art career and desire to be in a new, loving relationship was put aside as I continued to embrace an *attitude of latitude*, allowing my bubble of beliefs to move and expand while fearlessly throwing myself into the unknown world of healing arts.

Fast forward from that dark night of my soul to the end of two very happy, peaceful, loving years for our family, I finally felt in full flow as I confidently and bravely followed my calling into the world of service. My son had been catching up with his life and was doing exceptionally well at school, excelling in art, music, and football. The biggest gift and joy had been watching him be able to concentrate enough to finally learn to read at eleven.

Suddenly, two years later, this pipe dream came to an end, and I found myself in my worst nightmare. Picture my dear son, now in his early teens, lying in a hospital bed fighting for his life with tubes attached to him all over his body after a massive tumour was removed from his brain. Now, imagine me completely drained once more of my confidence as a mother and not knowing what to do, angry as hell with God for reneging on the deal I had made. Standing in the middle of the huge buildings surrounding the children's hospital, crying my eyes out, I blasphemed and yelled at God, so angry and completely lost, and feeling desperately alone and forsaken as I completely abandoned my faith in God—and myself!

Then, unexpectedly, I felt all anger and resentment drain through my body into the earth and an energy rising in me. There was a deep knowing that there was no way I could move forward and manage my life without my faith! This time there were no deals, no conditions. This time I vowed to unconditionally love and believe in my Creator, whom I later came to know as the Great Spirit, and I knew in my heart that somehow we would get through this heart-wrenching time.

As the weeks and months passed, and I took my son to professional and alternative healers of one sort or other every second day, it became clear he had had a stroke and the fine motor skills in his right hand had been irreparably damaged. He could no longer pursue anything he had previously excelled in and loved, and my heart went out to him. Not only had the operation failed to remove all of the tumour, a series of MRI scans showed it was returning at a rapid rate. Two years on when it was clear the tumour was becoming dangerous, the surgeon urged us to allow him to operate again, this time to take all of the tumour by cutting through a major artery and vein that would leave my son without memory of his former life and everyone in it. Can you imagine having to make that decision?

My confidence in myself once again plummeted, and though I knew the surgeon was highly skilled and competent, I was filled with fear and doubt. This lack of confidence in myself didn't last long, as I had become far more resilient from all the inner work I had undertaken during my studies, and there was so much to do and be ready for. Somehow, in agreement with my son and his father, the decision was made to go ahead with the operation, and I went about preparing my son exceptionally well to be strong in body, mind, heart, and spirit for the massive journey he was embarking on.

I remember so clearly now standing next to my son with the surgeon as he was preparing us both for the operation. He had gently guided us to say goodbye to each other as our relationship would never be the same again. Almost the whole of my immediate family had travelled large distances to visit my son in the hospital earlier that day and, after saying their sad farewells, they were gathered in a nearby park holding the energy and praying for him. As I stood there listening to the doctor describe his plan for the operation, a familiar feeling filled my energy field, and I knew to take a moment of silence and listen. A voice inside of me guided to me to ask the question: *"Doctor, do you ever follow your intuition when operating?"* A huge wave of resistance came over me at first hearing this question, as I was programmed to obey those in position of authority, but the question wouldn't go away, and it took all the courage I could muster to finally ask it out loud. It would eventually steer the path ahead of me in a completely new direction. The surgeon came back with words similar to: *"If you are asking me if I might change my mind during the operation, then no, I don't follow my intuition. I won't be changing my plan."*

Despite everything, my son and I were both at peace and after saying our final goodbye, my brave son was wheeled into surgery. Nine hours passed and in that nine hours I didn't move out of waiting room, spending every moment in prayer. My son's father and my close friend, Margaret, shared the agonising journey of waiting with me. Finally, the doctor came out to tell us the operation had finished, and he looked at me intensely, saying, *"I have something to tell you. For the first time in my life I didn't follow my plan, and instead I followed my intuition, which told me your son was too young to be affected in this way."* He went on to explain his astonishment in finding the hole left under the metal cap from the last operation had completely grown over, which prompted him to change his mind, as it indicated my son could heal himself. He said that he had removed as much of the tumour as he could and that there was nothing more he could do. The doctor was clearly out of his comfort zone and in unfamiliar territory.

Though at first feeling overwhelmed and not sure what do next, I began to develop greater trust in the unknown, understanding that anything is possible if you are open to it. I also realized that my inner guidance could be relied upon, if only I maintained faith in myself and the higher power guiding me and my son, and allowed space and latitude for big dreams to manifest.

The next few years were not particularly easy by any means, but they were filled with continuous synchronicity and healing adventures, including a miraculous healing journey my son and I took to Uluru, a beautiful sacred site in Central Australia (also known as Ayers Rock). I followed one sign after another as my son stepped into his healing power, and I could gradually let go and let higher powers lead the way. Our Uluru story needs more space than I have here to be told fully. Twenty-five years later, I am incredibly grateful and blessed that my son is alive—by the grace of a power greater than is possible to fathom. Though not always well, he is living a very simple, healthy, beautiful life close to Mother Nature and in service to humanity and the planet in his own special way. He has taught me far more about walking humbly and gracefully through life's challenges than I have ever taught him. There have been no more deals, and far less doubt. Recently I have been incredibly blessed to have found the love of my life, and we are bringing to life every day our combined beautiful dreams of continuing to serve the community and humanity with open, loving, and peaceful hearts and minds.

The Doubter still functions well in my most vulnerable moments. However, I have developed some wonderful ways to manage this destabilising archetype. The Victim has long been put to rest, and the Co-Creator, Mentor, and Spiritual and Peaceful Warriors are almost always at the forefront of my inner world archetypes these days. What I have come to realize more than anything is that not everyone in my close circle can meet me where I am, and I have the right to resist other people's projections and defend my dreams. I have long known that help from otherworldly guides and etheric helpers is always at hand. Here are a few of the ways that have been most helpful for me over the years in reclaiming and rebuilding the confidence to live a spirited and fulfilling life:

- Know thyself! (Socrates). Master your self-awareness and energy by uncovering and reclaiming your unique, innate gifts that you were born with, highlighting the values and positive traits of others of significance to you to assist you to expand in consciousness and confidence. Try these exercises to help with this:

    o *Examine and list the archetypal energies and values you are currently in alignment with, and decide if they are serving you. If not, then feel free to call in new archetypal energies more in line with the truth of who you are, and commit to other values.*

> o *Examine your ancestry and list the archetypal energies and values of those in your lineage whose strengths you admire and wish to awaken in your own soul's consciousness. Repeat this exercise with anyone you may have in mind whose qualities you aspire to gain in yourself.*
>
> o *Write a list of all the animals you love and their characteristics that you admire, and look for those traits that you share or wish to embrace.*

- Take time to identify, get to know, and follow the voice of your intuition. A wonderful way to practice this is to, upon waking, take time to vision your day unfolding and notice if your intuition interrupts to caution you or remind you of something.

- Be brave, speak your truth, and walk authentically in safe spaces until you feel you are able to relax and do this more naturally.

- Be humble and admit compassionately to yourself when you are feeling powerless, tracking this feeling back to the most significant imprint where the pattern of powerlessness first began. You may do well to have a professional guide you on this deep journey; however, you can journal your way through this passage as well. Your quest is to:

> o *Track the energy you are feeling to a time in the past when you supressed your feelings and swallowed your words.*
>
> o *Travel back in time to that wounded part of yourself that is sitting in the World Below, in a dark place.*

- o *Bring that part into the light and invite in a wise ancestor to sit with that part of you, your inner child, or inner wounded archetypal self.*
- o *Take some time to listen to and hold space for all the supressed feelings of that time to rise and be felt, acknowledged, and validated. This compassionate, loving process will transform all dark and dense energy into self-love and light.*

- Stretch and find the courage to ask for help when you need it. This help may come from your inner-world spirit guides, especially guides from the angelic realms and animal spirit guides who are always willing to help and guide you.

- Turn to tried-and-true creative slogans and affirmations to support you in moments of low self-confidence, procrastination, indecision, and entrapment. Try these to guide and motivate you into taking latitude by pushing boundaries and keeping you in positive motion:
  - o *A stitch in time saves nine—give up procrastination and strike while the iron is hot!*
  - o *First things first!*
  - o *Easy does it—one day, one moment, one step at a time.*
  - o *You've got this!*
  - o *What would I love to do right now?*
  - o *It is my birthright to shine!*
  - o *The Universe has my back! I have my own back!*
  - o *I believe in myself and trust in my journey.*

- Look at dominant attitudes and beliefs—both negative and positive—that you are in alignment with. Track where they have come from and transform them if they no longer serve you. Here are some examples of attitudes that will assist you in elevating and expanding in consciousness and confidence:

o *An attitude of latitude, which gives you permission to move and stretch beyond previous limits.*

o *An attitude of gratitude for all things great and small.*

o *An attitude of abundance in all areas of life—for body, heart, mind, and spirit.*

o *An attitude of loving-kindness towards self and others.*

o *An attitude of graceful self-acceptance of things you cannot change.*

o *An attitude of mindful action to change the things you can.*

o *An attitude of acting on your intuition immediately.*

• Embrace your role and responsibility as a Co-Creator of your dreaming by confirming trust in your soul's plan, and at the same time, claiming your right to be free of energies that bind you in depleting ways and cause you to lose confidence and trust in yourself. Cord-pulling is a safe, gentle, and powerful way to do this. Try this:

o *Decide on people and past situations (which I will now refer to as 'the other') that bind you to the past and are not in alignment with your new way of walking.*

o *Go into a contemplative, higher 'inner sacred space,' and call in the other whom you wish to release from.*

o *Place the other in a circle of light and create a sphere of rainbow coloured light above them, or the situation.*

o *Locate in your body any cords between you and the other.*

o *Firmly pull these out and plug them into the sphere of light above.*

o *Say the following: "Thank you for all the goodness our connection has brought and I now release any negative cords that bind us, for the highest good of all let this be so, and so it is! Thank you, thank you, thank you."*

o *Breathe the other out of your inner world with gratitude in your heart for the completed journey, and do not bring them to mind for the next few days, or at all, so as to stay disconnected. You can also replace the cords with coloured light beams of love if you wish to stay connected in more positive and loving ways.*

Conclusion

Thank you for joining me here and on this greater journey of retrieving the unique and rich gifts you are blessed with, and for allowing me to share my gifts with you. Please know that the key to feeling confident on your path is to *know thyself*: to find ways every day to lovingly affirm how brave you are to be stretching and growing in love and light in so many courageous, trusting ways. Part of the journey toward walking confidently in the world is not only to know yourself, but also to trust yourself and the path that has called you in *spirited, full-hearted ways*.

While it is always wise to ask for and listen to counsel, be sure to choose your mentors wisely, and know that the greatest counsel can come from a sound, practiced connection with the great source of light of which you are a divine spark—the Creator God, Source of your own understanding.

"Your success will be determined by your own confidence and fortitude."

~ Michelle Obama

CHAPTER NINE

---◦◦◦◦---

A Journey of Self-Discovery Through Intuition, Authenticity, and Faith

By Oksana Aya

Uprooted

I remember June 24, 2020, like it was yesterday. I felt like a flower uprooted from the soil of my identity, torn from the familiar and thrust into the unknown, pulled out with all its roots that went deep. This was the day I moved to the U.S.A., "the land of opportunity," leaving behind all I thought I knew and loved in Ukraine. I was 15. But I would come to learn that sometimes, being uprooted is the first step toward discovering the strength of your roots.

Do you remember when you were 15 years old? You finally began to think you had some things figured out, maybe even caught a glimpse of who you were or might become, even if just a sliver. You had your group of friends, favorite places to go, foods to eat, and things to do. You were eager to grow up and be independent—hoping to be successful, confident in your steps in life, and maybe even happy.

Well, all of that felt ripped away from me. At least, that's how it seemed then.

I thought to myself, Dang (in Ukrainian, obviously), *I felt like I just started to get a grip on things, and now what? Is it really as good as they show it on TV? Am I going to live the life of Carrie Bradshaw from Sex and the City? ...But what if I can't thrive in this new land? I can barely speak the language... They'll probably laugh at me! What if I'm not happy there? What if I can't become the person my parents dream of me being in this so-called land of opportunity?*

My mind and heart were fully flooded with terror, anxiety, and helplessness. You can imagine how jarring this kind of upheaval was for a teenager. It wasn't just a move to another school, town, or even the same continent! This was moving oceans and seas away from everything familiar—away from *me.*

Fast-forward to 2024. How did that happen? How many marvelous adventures and intense roller coaster rides have I been on so far? What about you? Life has been a constant dance between chaos and stillness, each moment demanding a deeper connection to my authentic self.

The outer and inner worlds seem to demand more of us, asking us to be stronger yet gentler, more confident yet humble, truly authentic yet not self-important! I certainly have had—and continue to have— a battle with these challenges. Then, as I was in the middle of heavy times, I was called to write about building self-confidence. *What? Is this a joke? God? Universe? Christ? Mary? ...hello?* I couldn't believe it! Me? Writing about building self-confidence? Who am I? A river of self-doubt filled my body.

Eh, why not? After all, my life has been pretty incredible (in both good and challenging ways), and the adventure of self-exploration continues. Doesn't the journey matter more than the destination?

What is self-confidence? How does it look in your life? It's a wonderful quality to have—you might even say it's essential—but it's often elusive. It's the belief in one's abilities, decisions, and worth—a foundation for achieving goals, building meaningful relationships, and facing life's challenges with grace. And I had to achieve this in a country where I was a stranger? With a permanent accent?

The transition was anything but easy. I vividly recall my first day of school (10th grade, Lord have mercy!), walking into a classroom where every word spoken felt alien. Conversations swirled in a language I didn't yet understand, and I felt a gnawing sense of inadequacy. Social interactions, once natural, now felt like monumental tasks. I questioned whether I was good enough to fit into this new world, whether I was smart enough to learn the language, and whether I'd ever find my place. My stomach was tied in knots, and I could barely take deep breaths. I felt increasingly self-conscious. I always worried about saying the wrong thing. One day, I asked my classmate for a "rubber" instead of an eraser, and everyone thought the new girl was asking for a condom. Was I trying too hard? Did I sound ridiculous when I tried to speak? These questions eroded my confidence and made me hesitate to leave my comfort zone.

I remember one history class like it was yesterday. Our homework was to write a letter to the people of the country as the President of the United States. I always loved to write, so I saw this as an exciting and challenging task—to pour my heart onto the paper in another language!

The day to read the presidential speeches arrived. The class was at 10 a.m.—that's how vividly I remember it. Normally, I liked it when the teacher rolled in the TV on a stand to show us clips or documentaries, but today I couldn't care less. I was determined to be brave and read my speech out loud. As the class went on, I raised my hand higher and higher, almost jumping out of my chair, trying to make eye contact with the teacher. I felt so confident that I had written a truly beautiful and inspiring piece. I couldn't wait for everyone to hear it—knowing it might reflect the depth and wisdom of my heart and maybe even the heart of where I came from.

At last, her gaze stopped on me. She paused for a few seconds, smiled, and said, *"You want to read a presidential speech? With your accent? Ha-ha-ha, honey! You could never be the president of this country. You weren't even born here!"*

Her words felt like a painful branding. I've never forgotten it. Sure, I knew I could never become the U.S. President, nor would I want to, but how could she be so insensitive and belittling? She was an adult, after all.

Building Resilience through Struggle

Over time, the very struggles that made me feel insecure shaped my resilience. Small victories began to add up as I pushed myself to learn the language and adapt to my new environment.

I remember the first time I held a full conversation in my new language—it was clumsy, but it was mine. Moments like these showed me that confidence wasn't about being perfect; it was about showing up and trying, even when the odds felt stacked against me.

The move taught me that discomfort is often the starting point for growth. It forced me to find strength I didn't know I had, and while I didn't realize it then, these experiences planted the seeds of self-confidence that would later bloom.

I often reminded myself of the story of a crab. As the crab grows, its shell—the home that once protected it—becomes more and more uncomfortable and constricting, to the point where it hurts and threatens to crush the crab. What will the crab do? Remain in the uncomfortable, but familiar, solace of an old shell, or break free, leaving the shell behind to grow a new, larger, and stronger one? The crab frees itself! And so must I. I strive to remember to free myself from the grip of deadly stagnation and old behavior patterns.

The Influence of Family Dynamics

Aside from mean teachers and bullying peers, our particular family dynamics heavily influenced us from a young age. Parents, siblings, and other family members played a significant role in shaping our belief in and acceptance of *self*. Even though these people love us, care deeply for our well-being, and want the best for us, their love often comes paired with a certain level of criticism.

The critiques could range across various areas—our appearance, our choices, and even the way we express ourselves. While criticism usually comes from a place of good intentions (though not always, unfortunately), it can create a lingering need to seek validation and acceptance from others. Many of us have constantly sought approval, hoping that praise would finally quiet our inner doubts and struggles. I was certainly no exception.

As much as I wanted to feel free, I often found myself looking for that invisible nod of approval. But the truth was, no amount of external validation could fill the void left by my lack of self-assurance and faith in my authentic being.

Breaking Free from the Need for Approval

As I grew older, I realized that living for approval was exhausting and unsustainable. A pivotal moment came during a desperate search to answer the question: *Who am I?* This happened while I was navigating a very difficult romantic relationship—the kind that alienated me from friends and especially family. It was a relationship that further eroded my sense of self-worth and belonging. Many of us have experienced "one of those."

My beautifully courageous moment of clarity came during a 10-day self-discovery trip to Cusco, Peru, in March 2014, right after I turned 29.

It was terrifying yet exhilarating and liberating at the same time. That trip marked the beginning of a profound realization: the only approval I truly needed was my own. The only voice I should honor is the voice of my heart and inner guidance. The only thing I need to do is keep going, keep growing, and keep getting clearer about who I am and how I want to show up in this world.

This shift didn't happen overnight, but it marked the start of a deeper journey toward self-acceptance—and, with it, confidence.

Discovering Intuition, Faith, and Authenticity

As I navigated the challenges throughout the years, I turned inward for guidance more often. One discovery led to another, synchronicities emerged, and I could not deny the presence of something sacred and magnificent guiding me—if I paid attention, that is! Intuition and spiritual faith were key elements that allowed these transformative forces into my life.

Intuition became a powerful guide in my decision-making. Each time I trusted that inner whisper, I stepped closer to a life that felt aligned with my true purpose. At first, I doubted this quiet inner voice. Was it reliable? Could I trust it? But as I listened more closely, I realized that my intuition often led to better outcomes than external advice ever had. My confidence began to grow as I trusted my inner knowing.

My grad school letter of intent was a wonderful and inspiring example of this. I had always been a much better "doer" than a multiple-choice test taker. When I graduated from nursing school, my GPA was not optimal, making it difficult to get into graduate school. But I felt a strong calling—I knew deep within my soul that this was what I was meant to do: to serve humanity in the field of healthcare and to be a facilitator of healing and transformation. So, I decided to apply!

Despite many suggestions about how well-written, perfectly stated, and astute my letter of intent should be, I wrote it my way: heartfelt, raw, brutally honest, and transparently authentic. To my surprise and joy, my authenticity spoke louder than any GPA, and I was accepted.

For much of my life, I thought confidence was something you gained by fitting in—by meeting expectations, saying the right things, or presenting the "right" image. But over time, I realized that the more I tried to mold myself to others 'standards, the more disconnected I became from my true self—ironically, the more my confidence suffered. Many of us wear masks in our personal and professional lives to meet the expectations of others, often forgetting to stop and ask ourselves: *What do I want? Who am I beneath all this?*

One exhausted evening, I stepped into a hot shower and began contemplating these questions. As I relaxed in the steamy water, I suddenly felt as though everything around me was muted and ceased to exist. In that moment, I deeply understood that confidence is a facade anyway. Real, grounded confidence is built through the courage to show up vulnerable and unapologetically yourself.

If I allow myself to be true to who I am—authentic in every way possible, with clarity in my thoughts and actions—then there is truly no one else exactly like me. And if I believe that we are all here for a mission and a purpose, then it is my responsibility to be who I truly am. It is yours too.

Authenticity is truly magnetic—it draws people in and builds genuine connections. Most of us can sense when someone is being "real," so to speak. Authenticity attracts people, not perfection. And what could be the downside? Attracting those who appreciate your true nature and weeding out the rest? That doesn't seem like a bad bargain to me.

Another important aspect of confidence for me is clarity. When I have clarity of thought or emotion, I feel much more confident about making decisions and taking certain steps. Yet, developing clarity requires walking the path of self-exploration and discovering our true nature.

The arduous task, then, is not to build self-confidence but to continuously discover my true nature with perseverance and courage. The obstacle to overcome is the fear of being judged or misunderstood. It's fear that keeps us away from the marvelous discoveries of self.

This leads to another question: *How do we overcome the fear of being our true, authentic selves?*

As I sit here writing, hoping to share my heart and experiences with you as meaningfully as I can, I can't help but reflect on the endless nature of this journey. New obstacles and challenges will continue to arise. Each challenge is an invitation to deepen our faith, honor our intuition, and embrace the authenticity that makes us whole. This provides us with opportunities to grow and evolve even further. After all, we are infinite beings, and the journey we find ourselves on only expands and deepens.

"Believe in yourself and all that you are. Know that there is something inside you that is greater than any obstacle."

~ Christian D. Larson

CHAPTER TEN

---∘◦✑◦∘---

Waking up from a Nightmare

By Julian Mann

My vision blurred, my head foggy. A tender pain ached my heart. I focused on the breathing exercises I had learned in an attempt to keep the rising panic at bay.

I was on a train from London to Manchester. I thought I could handle it, but the effects of my depression were a lot stronger than I had realized. Even though it was a simple journey that I had done many times before, I didn't think I could finish it. I just felt so ill and so drained.

After 27 years of marriage, I was recently divorced. The process had been deeply painful for me and full of conflict. My world had fallen apart. I missed my little girl, who I used to tuck in every night. The solicitors' fees were far beyond what I could afford, especially in my depleted state. Eventually, the constant distress led to a breakdown, and I was diagnosed with depression with a total loss of confidence.

Until a few years before, I had worked for years as a horticultural therapist and was fully aware that depression could limit cognitive function and severely impact motivation. I had become proficient at going into the wards and gently persuading those who were hurting too badly to get out of bed, and come with me for a gardening session, knowing it would boost their morale.

But I had never experienced it from the other side. I had spent the better part of the past two weeks in bed, my body too fatigued to move. I couldn't concentrate or focus on simple tasks, my nerves were frayed, and I suffered from a constant dull pain in my chest. My counselor had gone over a safety plan with me to reduce the risk of me being able to act on my suicidal thoughts. I'd moved back in with my parents at 52 years old and I had no money. My confidence had hit rock bottom.

However, I started to feel a little bit better and was touched when my sister offered to buy a car for me to share with my brother-in-law. It was like a glimmer of hope because it represented something good happening in my life. But the car was in Manchester and my brother-in-law was unavailable, so I needed to get on a train from Hertfordshire to King's Cross station in London and then get the train up to Manchester. That's a three-hour train ride there and a four-hour drive back.

I really wanted the car and was so grateful to my sister for buying it that I felt picking it up was the least I could do. Looking back, I now realize I was expecting too much of myself and I don't think my family fully understood just how ill I was.

So, when the day came, I got myself up and got on the train. I had only been up and about for a few days, and I remember that I did not feel so good, but I forced myself to get it done, figuring that being active would make me feel better anyway.

I made it to King's Cross Station and got on the fast train to Manchester. As the initial focus to get onto that train faded, I began to notice those feelings of dull pain and, with it, the now all-too-familiar fogginess in my brain. I couldn't concentrate, I became disoriented. I didn't know where I was. I remembered breathing techniques where you breathe out for longer than you breathe in to stimulate a sense of safety. I focused on breathing and regained some small sense of myself. But this was all I had to hold onto. My head cleared enough for me to remember I needed to get off at Manchester, but I didn't know where I was on the journey, how long I had been on the train, or when it would arrive.

It's humbling to realize that as a grown man who had been on trains thousands of times in my life, I really had no confidence that I would be able to complete the journey successfully. But that is how debilitating mental illness can be.

Then the voice came over the Tannoy announcing how many stations were left and I knew there was about an hour to go. As I became more centered, my mind moved onto the next concern. Here I was, barely able to cope with the train, yet on the other hand, I would have to find the auction house where I would pick up the car and drive it two hundred miles home.

Through the dull pain and fog, I thought to myself, 'How the hell am I going to handle this? This is a nightmare!' Then another voice came through, like a ray of sunshine that penetrated the darkness: 'If you are having a nightmare, you need to wake up.'

At that moment, I had an insight that the main cause of my illness had been holding onto a deep sense of pain and resentment at the injustice I had experienced. I had given everything to make my marriage work. I worked myself to the bone; I did everything I could to make us secure as a family. And I had failed utterly. In fact, I never had a chance. Believe me, I tried. Time and time again I got up from defeat and resolved that I would go again, I would never give up. But I had fallen one too many times. I lost all my confidence in myself as a result.

I suddenly realized the deeper meaning of forgiveness. I had read about it many times and thought I understood, but in the face of personal loss and struggle, I had not been able to let go of my anger. It ate away at me like a cancer until I finally caved in, despair overwhelming me, and fell into depression.

As I realized what had happened in my life, I inevitably became very angry, and this became the motivation I needed to leave a bad situation. However, it was also highly toxic and detrimental to my peace of mind. Leaving that situation also meant dismantling the life I had worked so hard to build; it meant accepting that my best had not been good enough. It meant letting go of a dream I had desperately wanted to realize that had never happened. I would need to let go of my anger before I could truly build an authentic sense of self-belief and trust again.

The anger manifested as conflict, a mental game of cat and mouse: You push me, so I push back. You hurt me, so I will defend myself even if that means hurting you. Not to mention a deep sense of offense at what I saw as the hurtful lies and constant manipulation I had been so unfairly subjected to. And so, this became my reality. It appeared that I had lost everything, and the pain this caused led to even greater anger. Then, every time I had a communication about my divorce, it began to move into feelings of fear and panic.

I had spent years following the three principles of Mind, Thought, and Consciousness, but I had recently left this understanding to explore other philosophies, and one aspect of this was to turn toward every aspect of your experience to look for the lesson in it. The general gist would be that our being here is miraculous, and, therefore, all experience is a gift if we can let go of our judgment of it. However, I have since realized that turning towards our most negative experiences and embracing them holds no value.

If I am holding a jar of toxic sludge, the best thing I can do is pour it away; after finding a way to safely dispose of it, of course. If I were to say, 'Wow, a jar of toxic sludge, what a gift of experience, how amazing!' and then hold the jar to my lips and drink it, I would not only be insane, but I would also fall very ill. There is no gift in toxic sludge; it is poison plain and simple.

If our thoughts are toxic sludge, we need to learn to pour them away. We can do this when we realize that toxic sludge, or negative thoughts, hold no value and will only hurt us.

Our feelings tell us everything we need to know about whether our thoughts are healthy or unhealthy. Learn to trust them. It's so simple, yet we struggle to accept it. We are afraid that if we ignore our negative feelings, we will be taken advantage of. This is only due to a misunderstanding of how to use negative thought. If the accompanying feeling is not so good, then the thought is telling us that following that path will lead to problems, so we need to make another choice. Recognizing these feelings builds a sense of trust within yourself, increasing your confidence.

What happened to me on that train as my insight unfolded was that I realized firstly that holding on to conflict, anger, fear, and resentment was the key cause of my depression. Second, I remembered what I had seen some years before, that all of my feelings and experiences come to me via my thoughts. All experience is thought in motion, brought to life via consciousness. I realized I could choose differently. I do indeed have freedom of thought; we all have this. If I can't see this at the moment, that's okay. The main thing is that I know life and experience come from thought and if I am lost in painful thoughts, I just can't see the sunlight on the other side of the clouds. I always have the power to let go of painful thoughts, even if I can't see how in the moment.

We can choose our thoughts.

We may not be able to see it, but we are always choosing our thoughts. By that, I mean that thoughts come to us all the time, some we discard, and some we choose to make real. Before you go judging yourself for not being able to choose good thoughts or rejecting what I am sharing because it sounds untrue, please just take a moment to think about what I am saying.

Is it possible to have an experience of any kind without a thought? Is it possible to be aware of that thought without being conscious? Is it possible to be conscious without a mind?

This is how I am interpreting the three principles to share this story.

This insight on that train was so powerful that I began to feel better straight away. I was still tired, and my heart still felt tender, but the fog began to lift, and I was able to make my way to the auction house and drive back home successfully.

I am so grateful I was able to come back to this understanding. In realizing the role of thought in our experience, we can indeed wake up from even our worst nightmares. Confidence becomes a natural state of being. A way of looking into this more deeply to see the malleable and dreamlike nature of our life experience is to explore the oneness of life.

If this makes sense, then that's wonderful, but if it doesn't ring true for you then don't feel you have to go with it! We often hear spiritual teachings speak of the oneness of life. My limited understanding of this tells me it is something we need to realize from within and that words can only point the way.

Sydney Banks often talked about how everything stems from one infinite formless energy. Everything, whether in form or formless, is this one energy. Everything in form is the one formless energy experienced as that form via the power of thought. That is why Sydney Banks described life as a divine dream. Because everything in life is thought.

That is why if you find yourself having a nightmare, you can wake up. Because life is a dream of thought, and if this is realized, we can choose a different dream. The greater mind as the creator of all things creates life via divine thought. As individuals who are the one divine thought in motion, we have our personal thoughts, and I see these as reflections of the divine thought. As there is only one energy there is only one thought, and all our individual experiences and realities are this one divine thought in motion.

In Part Two, I will point you toward a fundamental truth: Self-confidence is not something we need to build; it is our natural state of being. That means self-confidence already exists within us.

If we do not feel confident, it means we have forgotten who we are, but we don't need to "find" this confidence because we already have it. We need only uncover it.

Part Two

If all our experiences and feelings come to us via thought, then confidence, or the lack of it, must also come to us via thought. If I think I am confident, then I will feel confident, and that will be my experience. If I do not think I can do something and I do not think I am confident, then again, this will be my experience.

It's important not to confuse confidence with knowledge and education.

For example, I have several qualifications in horticulture and landscaping, so I have an extensive education in my chosen field. I've built hundreds if not thousands of patios. So, of course, I am confident in my ability to lay a patio. However, I have little experience in computer programming, so I am not confident that I could create an AI algorithm to predict weather patterns affecting climate change over the next twenty years.

This is only logical and does not indicate whether I am a confident person or not. The question is: if I have adequate interest and access to the right information, do I believe I could successfully learn a new skill, such as computer programming, and produce competent results?

If I am confident in my abilities to learn, grow, and succeed, then I am a confident person. If I am not confident in my abilities, then I am not a confident person.

It's also helpful not to confuse our natural talents and gifts with our worth as a person. I may have no interest whatsoever in computer programming, so it would not indicate I am not confident if I do not think I could learn about computer programming; it just means I know myself and would be better off directing my energies to areas that interest me.

I remember when my daughter was born. She was so beautiful and tiny. She also knew nothing of this world. We put little mittens on her hands so she would not scratch herself because she had not yet learned what her hands were for.

As babies, we must learn everything—even how to sleep. Babies have no concept of being confident or unconfident. They simply learn to interact with the world they find themselves in and eventually, they master how to use their bodies. As they grow up, they learn how to interact socially and become more refined people.

Essentially, we come into this world with an innate confidence. There is no self-judgment, only trying and learning through experience. Children find joy in the process of experiencing and learning. Everything is a magical moment. Can you find that joy within yourself? I promise it never left you.

With that in mind, logically, we must have learned to feel unconfident through our experiences. At some point, a negative experience—where we were judged and told we were in some way not good enough—made us forget our natural, innate state of confidence, as it became obscured by fearful thoughts that we might be in danger of being judged. And so, we lost our connection to our confidence and became afraid to try new things.

To me, trauma is any painful experience that causes us to make up a set of beliefs about reality to protect ourselves from experiencing that pain again. In many cases, these beliefs become ingrained at an unconscious level, meaning they become invisible to us.

If you are reading this book, it must mean that you are ready to look at how to become more confident. This may well mean that what was invisible to you will become visible. When it does, you will be able to see that this is just a collection of old thoughts based on your memories of past events now long gone. When you see this, you will see that these beliefs are no longer true, and you will be able to drop them.

I must also point out that it is possible to drop these limiting beliefs without even becoming aware of them if you gain a deep enough insight. Once again, it always comes down to the fundamental truth that we have the power to drop thoughts.

Think once more of the baby. This was you once, embracing life. Loving every moment of your experience. As a baby, you had no painful memories, and you lived fully in the Now.

What are these painful memories of a now non-existent past other than thoughts? They do not exist in any other way. All experience can only come to us via thought. As a baby you were completely free, that freedom is your birthright. If you stop and think about it, Now is the only moment that exists. There is no future, there is no past, there is only now.

The past exists only in thought via memory. It no longer exists.

The future that we spend so much time worrying about also does not exist except in our thoughts.

When we realize the Now, we return to our natural state of well-being—our natural state of confidence. Before we learned another way of looking at life that is not true.

Something we innocently took on to protect ourselves, but that also holds us back and covers up our true magnificence.

How do we recognize the Now? You don't need to look for it. When you see it, you will know.

Remember earlier in the chapter when we viewed our experience of life as being a dream, the experience of which is brought to us via thought? This dream then operates within the boundaries of time and space, meaning that time is also a part of the dream brought to us via thought. Can you reach beyond thought into the Now? Authentic confidence is in the Now. Present-moment awareness is where all life is.

If everything is one infinite energy, if infinity is true, and it is, this means that there can be no beginning, and no end, and so time is an illusion. Now is the only moment that exists. It's not even a moment. It is just Now.

It is accessed in a moment of quietness—beyond thought, beyond form. In the silence of our minds, we find the truth. I have been calling it "the Now," but you could also call it "love."

That is who we truly are. No need to try and be confident. Simply come into the present moment—and *be*.

Our lives are compelling and seem so real to us, but reality is not what it appears to be. Just as the sun appears to travel across the sky, we now know that while this appears to be happening, it is, in fact, the Earth moving around the Sun, not the other way around.

But in every moment, we have the power to realize our true nature. And in that moment of realization, the reality that once seemed so rigid becomes malleable and can change. Our truth is health, well-being, abundance, and confidence. This is who we are, but our dream, at times, becomes a nightmare.

It really is only a dream. And we have the power to change that dream if we can find a way to wake up. A key to waking up comes in a deeper discovery of the power held in our thoughts. You can work with your body, you can do breath work and any number of other things if you find them helpful, only you can know what is right for you. These can be effective ways of calming the mind through relaxing the body.

However, what I am pointing to is that behind it all, there is thought. Words are not adequate to explain thought, but they are what we have. Try to expand your parameters of what thought is to glimpse the truth, because even the slightest glimpse can change everything.

That's what happened to me on that train. I had one moment of connection, and one magical thought was all it took for me to come back from depression, from being unable to carry out even simple tasks to realizing my innate wellness. After losing all my confidence, after feeling like I had totally failed at life, after falling into deep despair and thinking about ways I could end my life, I was given a second chance. I rediscovered my confidence.

I truly believe every single person on the planet is a beautiful and unique expression of the divine. Each of us came to this planet with our own unique gifts, and it is a sad thing that the density of experience makes so many of us lose our way and lose our confidence.

You are valuable simply by the fact that you exist. You are part of the great wholeness, just as beautiful and worthy as anyone else, because there is no separation between any of us. We cannot be apart from life; we are life.

We will have difficult experiences throughout our lives. We will experience challenges that shake our confidence. But in those very difficulties lies the possibility of rising to new heights of confidence and living a more beautiful and joyful life.

My perspective is that I survived my darkest night. I found hope in my moment of deepest despair. I found the light when, before, all I could see was darkness. Now, I have a more profound sense of confidence than ever before in my life.

In learning to let go of my negative thoughts, my heart opened, and I found a deeper sense of love and understanding to guide me through life. I could do this as I realized my negative thoughts held no value whatsoever.

I saw that the people I was angry with were only doing what they knew how to do according to their level of consciousness, directing the thoughts they had available from that level of consciousness. I saw that it was the same for me. I found compassion, I found forgiveness. That is how I could wake up from my personal nightmare of depression.

If you are experiencing a nightmare, please take heart and know that this is just a phase in your life. Underneath all the pain, your light is still shining. You have the power to heal and realize yourself as a confident, powerful person. You can wake up; you are only dreaming. I hope this story and my perspective will help you to wake up. I say this with the greatest tenderness.

We are here living life together, growing and learning. We will have moments of glory and moments of darkness—that is the beauty of the human experience. We are naturally confident beings. When we realize we do have power, then we unlock a world of unlimited possibility.

Our possibilities are endless because we are endless. We are drops in the ocean of infinity. But that is our nature. We are infinity, even though we may be only a tiny drop in the great ocean. This means that we are without boundaries, without limitations. Any limitations we see are simply our thoughts about how life is. The good news is that there are an unlimited number of thoughts available. So, there are an unlimited number of possibilities available.

"The best way to gain self-confidence is to do what you are afraid to do."

~ Swati Sharma

CHAPTER ELEVEN

⸺∞◐✑◑∞⸺

Defining and Refining
Self-Confidence

By Kim Frazer

H ow often do you look outside of yourself for your self-confidence? A younger version of me would say, "Quite often…" Yet confidence is not about being fearless—it is about embracing the courage to show up fully, with imperfections and all, knowing that you are enough exactly as you are. Life educates us when we are willing to see the growth opportunities, which we only see when we are looking back versus forward. The moments when we form our beliefs begin as soon as we take our first breath.

And so my story begins.

It was a hot summer night. A bright red color softly spread over her young full lips. She was moving quietly from a girl's energy into that of a woman in a moment in time, it seemed. Her soft skin presented the flawless look of a beautiful palette that exemplified her youth. The long eyelashes pulled you in as she spoke, loud enough to always be heard and to bring others into her energy with her laugh. She was confident to be all she felt compelled to be as she presented what life contributed to her version of beauty.

She grew up in a family of five handsome brothers and a beautiful sister, looking up to others as she formed her own concept of confidence. Her sister was head cheerleader and homecoming queen—popular, beautiful, and loved by everyone that knew her. Her brothers were all so different, protective, and filled with action; there was never a dull moment in the house. Her father was a strong, opinionated presence, stoic yet loving unconditionally and always showing up for her and her family. His handsome and protective dad energy gave her a feeling and vision of what she would seek in the male figures in her life. Her mom was a pillar of beauty with a strong, nurturing, feminine energy. She taught her daughter how to cook, clean, care for herself, and be beautiful inside and out. She was the essence of a woman in all she did, and the girl would do her best to emulate her mama. Homemade dinners made it to the table at 5:00 p.m., her mother dressed prettily with hair and makeup done and a loving smile on her face for the family as she kept it all together.

With the strength and grace of these role models, the young woman would grow to be confident and strong, just like her amazing parents. Her family home was filled with the energy of family being together, roughhousing, having fun, eating homemade meals, and sharing lots of love. The imprints of impact were everywhere in her environment.

Looking confident was something she was good at; she caught the attention of others everywhere she went, her energy preceding her. Her attire was something many would take a second glance at as she pieced her outfits together with confident energy—*pow!* Leopard print, rhinestones, fringe, and flash caught people's attention as she walked into any room. She felt the beauty outside her compelling enough that it could expand into the successful life she longed for.

Longing to be the best version of herself that she could be, she continued to seek role models who would feed, encourage, and lift her along the way. So many people and situations enriched her sense of confidence as she journeyed through a successful modeling and sales career. The diamonds, awards, Cadillacs, and cash were all an outside reward for the belief she continued to find outside of herself. The relationships she fostered and the edification she found from mentors and men continued to give the praises that seemed to fulfill her. These praises helped her to feel worthy of living a life filled with empowerment.

Many powerful, conscious lessons would be born from this mindset. How do I know? Because that young woman was me.

Mastering the Release of "Outside In" to Drive Self-Confidence

My over-identification with performance led to perfectionism in my career mindset. It felt fulfilling and fun, while the values of creating my own family remained fleeting. Controlling my environment and relationships—controlling people to prevent them from trying to control me—kept me in a spin of avoidance and being controlled and controlling. This learned behavior was rooted in fear. My entire energy went toward creating financial independence and growing relationships that fostered what I could control—yet another illusion.

More often than not, this mindset was something I had to overcome. Control really is the opposite of allowance. Life is much lighter when we allow what is meant to flow in and what is meant to flow out. We learn in life that how we do one thing is how we do everything. Energy does not lie; it's either heavy or light. I have learned that my over-analyzing brain is usually not my friend. It works overtime, trying to figure this confidence thing out, especially when it comes to relationships.

Each of the long-term partners I picked had many great qualities and taught me many great lessons. As a teenager, I dated a man six years older who had a "no bull" attitude and was very rooted in his spirituality and who he was. He handled my wild young tendencies with such grace, teaching me unconditional love and friendship through all of my years of acting out. I grew to appreciate the roots of solid friendship and love we still have.

In my next long-term relationship, I experienced the intense passion and pain of loving someone who struggled with alcohol. The lessons on that journey expanded my ability to have compassion for putting up with someone who had an addiction. I also learned how strong I really was and how deeply I could love. I learned about codependence. I learned that changing another is never the job of me being confident; it is a growth opportunity to learn boundaries and surrender to change. The only one I can change is me. I like to think my inspiration, and my partner's readiness to stop drinking and become healthy, were brought on by our choice to go our own ways. I am grateful friendship remains.

The next person I dated was not emotionally available for a relationship, yet he taught me so much! Top of the list of lessons was to believe in myself again, after the blow to my self-worth that had occurred after dating an alcoholic. I learned to dream again, to live in excellence, and to be bold in all I am and do—to be all of me! I felt a kindred spirit with him even though our timing just didn't work out.

Reflecting on my most recent relationship, I learned so much. School is never out for a seeker. I learned about follow-through and what is possible when you are willing. I also learned about being spontaneous together. The relationship taught me vision and what it felt like to be spoiled; my partner also has a beautiful daughter, so I felt like we were a family. I learned that with complacency, things change over time. I learned that when communication is not strong between two people, and one is outgrowing the other, obstacles are created. Growing together is the only way for a relationship to flourish. The lesson to be true to myself continues to be revealed to me as I move forward on my journey. I continue to break through self-judgment and stay true to my path. Unconditional love is what remains. I learned that true best friendship and safety are what every solid relationship is built on.

Every relationship along my life path helped to shape my confidence—or so I thought. Finally, I had to become rooted in the idea and truth that those relationships were all signposts along the way, acting as mirrors to how I loved or did not love and respect myself. My character grew through these relationships, and every one of them brought me closer to my true self.

We all play a character in each person's story. I learned that confidence is never about another person; it is about me. When the student is ready, the teacher appears. The right people will always align.

My dad said that marriage would be the way a man would take care of me. This mindset came from a different era of thinking. While a partner adds value, it is not the value in its entirety. Happiness, learning, and growth are. My hyper-independence continued to be a protective mechanism to prevent anyone from getting close. This felt like strength when, really, what I was lacking was the ability to lower my guard and be vulnerable in a way that true confidence allows. My awareness of living "outside-in" brought validation to my soul until, one day, that thought process no longer worked. I realized I needed more. I simply needed progress, not perfection.

I now choose to grow into new levels of personal and professional expansion. Self-confidence is a choice based on what I believe about myself, not what someone else believes. When my feelings are based on what another does or doesn't do, I am off-center from creating my happiest and highest-vibe life. I am responsible for bringing my feel-good vibes to my life, and that starts by following my dream.

Self-Awareness and Alignment

Having control felt like confidence; it was familiar, running in the background of my life. *If I don't practice control, my vulnerabilities might be exposed*, I would think. But truly, you can only control yourself, not another person. Fighting to keep everything under control steals from you the joy of living your very existence.

Control is not love. It is an illusion, and surrendering it allows relief to flow into you. It is a practiced skill to love and live with an open hand of release. Being in control of your responses versus your reactions? That is peace.

Practice pausing when your first thought is to react. Do some deep breathing and stabilize your nervous system before responding in any situation. Get into your body. This was something I had to learn through the heartache of not pausing. I realized that people's points of view were simply their opinions, not a need to control me or for me to control them. Confidence is not control. Telling a new story allows a new life to unfold, and I am experiencing that now—wow, what a long lesson of such value!

What is in alignment will not be continually hard. Alignment feels magical, like an internal, confident smile inside out. Recognize where your external achievements potentially clash with your internal fulfillments, and trust that anything can change in a moment through awareness and choice.

Inner Trust and Self-Validation

The true mastery of confidence is in understanding that our energy leaks, and knowing where to stop the drain in our own energy field. When I put my self-confidence and self-esteem outside myself, how I feel is no longer my choice—it is now contingent on another person to fill my cup and make me feel good. It is my job to make myself feel good, so my outer world will reflect my inner world. Following the inner nudge of our dreams is a confident choice.

The concepts of self-confidence and follow-through are closely linked. Confidence and belief in ourselves add fuel to our journey; we must believe in our ability to "be" and bounce back each time we fall. This belief strengthens with repetition and grows from each experience. What we say to ourselves over and over becomes what we believe. When I allow myself to be solid in belief and in my thinking, my actions follow through. I've replaced the mindset of "fake it until you make it" with "feel it until you heal it and see it as you desire it to be, and know why you desire what you do. A great way to know is because it makes you feel a certain way." We must lean into what is light and lean away, in thoughts and actions, from what is heavy. Stretching our comfort zone consists of making little choices—one at a time—that stack up to the bigger feel-good moment.

When you tolerate low vibrational treatment from another person, a self-esteem and worthiness issue is at play. Work on your value and the engine that is rooted in self-worth and self-acceptance.

When you grow, you then have a choice to release past pain and celebrate your victories. Regardless of how amazing or difficult your growing-up years might have been, you can benefit from looking at your past and learning how to become better, not bitter, from it all. You may be a product of your past, yet you are not your past. Progress is accompanied by growth, and as you learn and grow, you have the conscious choice to pick what feels good to your heart and soul. You have the choice to recognize that hurting people hurt people, and become confident in knowing that their behavior is not personal. Lean into what feels good, lean back from what doesn't, and expand to your next level.

School is never out for the one who is committed to a life of self-improvement, self-forgiveness, and the awareness that all things come to you for you. If you choose to transfer outside-in living to inside-out living, everything becomes possible. Broken down, the word "impossible" becomes "I'm possible." What do you love about yourself in this moment? What you give your energy to will grow. Do you continually place your self-validation within you or outside of you?

We learn what self-confidence is by learning what it is not. I find it interesting that when we are most challenged to be in the confidence of our spirit, life brings what I like to call "opportunity moments." These are the moments filled with choices to go down the rabbit hole of all the reasons we don't "deserve" to be confident and create our best life, or choices to believe that we all deserve our best life if we choose it.

Conscious confidence is the new sexy. The first step to any change is being aware and choosing to say yes to you.

You can write your own story—literally. Writing has such power; it is a form of transferring your true dreams into print and then into the wheelhouse of creation. When your story moves to one of empowerment, alignment, and having the confidence to believe in yourself, the fun of manifesting truly begins. What are you placing outside of yourself that hinges on the level of your success in life? Recognizing this is your internal work. When you stop seeking confidence externally and trust the inside of you, things shift. Those experiences and people you are seeking are seeking you. Your only job is to be the confidence you wish to see; it is all within you and begins the moment you say yes, inside out, to you.

Making Dreams Come True

I said yes to myself when I allowed my dream of visiting Bali to come true. It was one that I had dreamed of for years and finally made a reality in 2024. The deeper dive in our life is when we look at the dreams we have within us that can become our reality if we plan our work and work our plan. I went in thinking of beauty, yoga, and retreat vibes, but what I found was so much more! I found the higher version of me and the opportunity to release past stories, release past pains, and create a new mindset and possibilities of dreams coming true, as long as I am breathing, it's not too late. What's meant for you will not pass you by.

As I soaked in the jungle sounds, scents, and sensory rich sights, I recognized the power of vision and seeing what could be before it became real. Before, when I was younger, I saw the power of external beauty, as the environment in Bali taught me, beauty is in all our senses—sight, smell, touch, hearing, and taste—and what creates our truth is our point of view about those things. Everything I experienced was richer in vibration and through my senses than I had imagined. The incense was sweet and clean, and the fresh air felt so crisp and sweet. The food was pure, colorful, and delicious. It enriched my soul to partake in the flavorful delights of such a culinary paradise. New experiences kept the adventure flowing in my taste buds. Soul food surrounded me.

The intensity of the raw rock walls lowered my barriers and surrendered my guarded self to the vast ocean. The bliss of the tropical water transmuted my fear to comfort as I swam with the manta rays and turtles and colorful fish. Grace and self-love washed over me as I hugged myself in the water above an eight-foot-wide manta ray—pure magic! That memory is a place I can return to if I feel anxiety trying to creep in. Nature is healing. Confidence displayed outwardly began at an inner, soul level of expansion through magical moments like these. As the waves rolled, I relaxed and released the strain of trying to float and allowed the water to wash over me. I no longer carried my pains like a badge of strength, but released them with the lightness of a child at play in the great outdoors. As the manta rays navigated the water with the flow of trust and ease, I saw that we have so much to learn from nature. Introspection and emotional healing are fostered in nature when we are willing to lean in.

Riding the Bali swings in my long flowing red dress was an image I had dreamed of for years, and the experience was everything and then some to what I had imagined. The freedom and broader perspective to swing high above the jungle and flowing waters filled me with the courage to explore any of my perceived limitations. And the kindness of the people and the calm presence of the culture helped me to recognize my unconditional love and joy for life. Being surrounded by a sisterhood of amazing women reminded me of the power of healing together while still on our own journeys—of the pure commitment to be our best selves through the journey of up-and-down releasing.

The Pyramids of Chi light and sound healing was one of my favorite activities, as the sound bowls, waterbed, and light and sound therapy journey were nothing short of a magical release. I was greeted in my meditation by my angels, my dad, my brothers, and by other loved ones who had passed over. They emitted pure love as I lay on the twin waterbed with tears rolling down my face, absorbing their reminders for me to trust my intuition and heart. In a time-traveling kind of way, I released all of my past pains into the ocean and felt a million pounds lift. It's hard to put the moment into words, yet it is so magical as I revisit it; I long to go back.

Being encouraged to do the uncomfortable builds our confidence. We recognize our beauty in and admiration for life in its ups and downs. I possessed a humble yet confident strength as I shared my Bali attire, which exuded outward confidence and bliss energy on my socials. My Bali family expanded my heart, soul, and existence, and we all felt the magic in each of our individual expansion journeys. Energy is contagious; ask yourself, "Is mine worth catching?" Lean into your "yes" energy and send love and light to the rest.

A reflection of your unique light and strength comes from within. It is about embodying a quiet power that uplifts rather than overshadows. I have found that true confidence doesn't seek to dominate; it seeks to illuminate. As you lean into this energy, remember that your light to overcome is limitless. By shining authentically, you give other people permission to do the same.

Following your bliss is confidence, and pressing through your fears to feel is brave. It is self-love. It is truly the conversations you engage in, the beliefs you foster, and the things you attach meaning to that contribute to confidence. If I can lean into this knowledge through all that I have learned, so can you. Remember who you are—the healed you, that is. Trusting your vision to step in and live in a world where everything becomes possible is a gift you give yourself and the world! What else is possible for you?

When you can release judgement, confidence remains for all you are and desire to be. The skill of growing better in communication and expanding into your grandest dream creates more fulfillment. Choosing to practice mindfulness is the key to true self-confidence. You deserve your dream as much as I do.

Comparison is the thief of joy, and competition is not between you and another person experiencing their dream life. It is really between the old version of you and the authentic new version of you that says, "Yes, I am creating my most confident self." When you focus on your unique dream and own your journey, with all its twists and turns, the magic transforms you—though in moments, not overnight. Your perception truly creates your reality, and you can trust yourself.

Solid Self-Growth

True self-confidence is a journey, a spiral upward that cultivates trust within yourself. As you master skills, embrace self-awareness, and align your actions with your values and dreams, you see that true self-confidence resides not in what you do but in who you are. Living from the inside out means discovering that your worth is truly untouched by failure or success. You can fail forward and learn to be present in each episode of love, loss, failure, and success. The most profound power comes from honoring your expressed, authentic self.

With this realization, confidence becomes unshakable—not because life gets easier but because you have found your strength within. You, my friend, get to own your path to becoming the most confident version of yourself and creating the dream given to you! Yes, you can! Allow confidence to be the energy and magic that transforms the world within you and around you. Lean in and find the pathway lit just for you. Living inside out is your light. Shine On!

"**Confidence isn't thinking you're better than everyone else. It's realizing you have no reason to compare yourself to anyone.**"

~ Maryam Hasnaa

CHAPTER TWELVE

One Door Closes, Another Opens

By Harita Gandhi-Kashyap

I moved to Melbourne from New Zealand in 2014 and met Hemant in April 2016—ironically, through shaadi.com. Hemant's family friend Raman had set up a profile for him and he expressed interest in me—later on, I realized it was Raman monitoring the page, and that he would later show Hemant other profiles. I got to know Hemant's family quite quickly into the relationship; I think I met them all by May.

His family made me feel so happy, and I thought I fit right in. There were no arguments, disagreements, or anything. They included me in everything they did, always inviting me to their house for dinner and to family functions. As someone who had no family in Melbourne, I was so happy I found someone with a welcoming family. I felt so confident and comfortable around them. Hemant has a sister two years younger than me, and I thought she would become the sister I never had, even though we have very different personalities. I had always wished I had a sister or female cousin close to my age, and I finally had it in her.

I thought of Hemant's mum as "my Melbourne mum" because my biological parents live in New Zealand. My Melbourne mum was much more traditional than my mum, given that she was from India and my mum was from New Zealand, but she had welcomed me into her life, family, and society, which I was so grateful for. For fourteen months, I truly felt like I had found my second family. I felt like I belonged, like I had found a home and people who loved me in Melbourne. Naturally, this made me feel confident in knowing I had people around me who loved me, despite living in a different country from my own family. Anyone who has moved away from home and their family would know how important it is to feel a sense of belonging when they are away from the people they love.

Hemant and I dated for just over a year before he proposed to me, the day before my twenty-ninth birthday in June 2017. The proposal was definitely a spectacular one. We went on a helicopter ride, while he had my closest friends and his family gather on St. Kilda beach holding a huge hand-painted sign that said, "Marry me." I was on top of the world and felt like the luckiest lady alive. His family seemed so happy for us, too, so I never suspected whether they actually liked me. They all hugged me, and we went out for brunch after the proposal. Hemant's mum even went as far as asking me to come over to her house in a few weeks, to have a party with her friends and show them the engagement ring.

Maybe I should've realized the party occurred only so she could show off the ring she had bought for me from India? I don't think it was about me at all, in hindsight. She was looking for compliments about the expensive ring she had bought (I don't know how much it cost, but I could guess by looking at it). But, during these happy moments, I was the happiest I had ever been in my life, and of course, that goes hand-in-hand with self-confidence.

I grew up being quite shy and reserved because I was always the odd one out in my extended family. All my cousins are much older or younger than me, so to fit in, I always joined the parents, aunties, and uncles. No one in my extended family knew how to relate to me, and I grew up having to be a people-pleaser to fit in. Later in life, I realized how much this had negatively affected my mental health and self-confidence, and why I always looked for external validation.

With Hemant's family, I felt like I wouldn't need to look anymore. I felt like I would have him, his sister, and their cousins, who were all a similar age to me and therefore relatable. A massive weight began to lift off my shoulders, because I felt like I would no longer be lonely in life.

I thought my new family was happy for us when we got engaged, but a few months later, Hemant told me he had wanted to propose during a holiday we took to Queenstown in March 2017—a few months earlier than when he actually proposed. He had booked the helicopter ride and planned how he wanted to propose before our trip, and had even told my best friend all about it to check that it would be what I wanted. But before we left for Queenstown, his mum had told him that he was not ready to get married and she refused to give him the engagement ring (which was in a safe at a bank that only she had access to). So, he had to cancel his initial proposal plans because he was not given access to the ring.

I felt like my world was crashing down when he told me this, because for the previous fourteen months, things had felt like they were too good to be true—and that's exactly what was happening. The "honeymoon phase" was officially over, and this was the reality. His mum had a big issue with me and wanted to postpone the engagement. From this day forward, I knew I had to be careful with my in-laws, and constantly reminded myself that I was not their daughter. My self-confidence crashed, and I constantly walked on eggshells, at risk of losing myself because my fiancé's family didn't accept me.

A lot of verbally and mentally abusive events occurred between this incident and our marriage, which I later realized were described by the term "narcissistic abuse." In the end, we got married as planned, in September 2018. I was already thirty and Hemant was thirty—not that age mattered, but we definitely weren't "too young or immature" to get married. I never received a logical explanation about why his mum wanted to postpone the wedding or why she had caused so many arguments with me in the fifteen months between the engagement and the wedding, despite me asking Hemant to arrange a time so I could talk things out with her. I felt like I was the only one being mature in this whole situation, but everything I did was wrong.

I was sick of putting my own needs aside for my mother-in-law's mood swings. We did everything the way Hemant's parents had wanted; even the date we got married was because that was the date his mum wanted, even though none of his family attended.

Hemant's dad rang him two days before the wedding saying he was no longer coming. My family travelled from overseas, but Hemant's family couldn't even drive half an hour down the road to attend our wedding. The father of Hemant's friend, Anuj, told us that Hemant's dad had taken the day off work to attend the wedding, but still didn't turn up. Two hundred people attended our wedding, but we kept looking at the door to see if his family would come. It remains the saddest day of my life. To this day, I haven't been able to look at our wedding photos. A pain like this is so hard to explain to people who haven't gone through it. Such an experience can completely drain your confidence, knowing you'd done everything you could to improve a relationship, putting your own needs aside. There is such a fine line between the two, but in the end, we need to remember to build ourselves up.

Hemant was invited to two family weddings after ours, but I wasn't. He attended one of them and later told me that so many people had asked him where I was, that he'd told them the truth: I hadn't been invited. He decided not to attend the second wedding because he couldn't be bothered acting happy at someone's wedding when his wife wasn't invited. While grateful for his decision, by this point, I had often thought about ending my life. His family was treating me like I didn't exist. This made me feel so isolated and lonely, especially since I had no family of my own in Melbourne, even though I knew Hemant was always there for me. There was a big emptiness in my heart, and his family couldn't see how they were hurting me.

May 2019

I gave Hemant's family until March 31 to talk to me. They didn't, so I resigned from work and moved back to New Zealand on May 10, when our apartment lease ended. Hemant hadn't booked his flight yet but moved in with his parents for six weeks to reconcile with them, hoping that they would improve and realize we were not lying when we said we would move to New Zealand.

During the six weeks that I was in New Zealand and Hemant was in Melbourne, his mum constantly tried to brainwash him. She told him that if he moved, my parents and I would control him and ruin his life. I'm not sure why she thought this, when she herself hadn't bothered attending her son's wedding. She even tried to cancel it. She constantly made it seem like we wanted something from her family, something materialistic. But that assumption did not make sense, considering my parents are self-made millionaires who retired in their fifties and own businesses and multiple investment properties. I had more than I needed from my parents, and we honestly didn't want or need anything from my husband's family except some basic respect. His parents never visited my parents in New Zealand to see where they lived or what type of life they had or how we grew up.

Hemant ended up moving to New Zealand in July 2019. His dad had promised to sell his car for him after he moved, but he never did. Just one more false promise. I was diagnosed with severe depression, anxiety, and PTSD by the time my husband reunited with me in New Zealand. I had a miscarriage in 2019, which doctors told me could have been caused by stress. I've also had Crohn's disease since I was eighteen; if I don't keep my stress under control, the condition can flare up and cause other issues. Case in point: I was soon diagnosed with endometriosis. I truly felt like my feelings had been forgotten and that I simply did not exist. I constantly wondered if I should just end my life and make the world easier for all these people since I seemed to be ruining their lives.

During this period, I learned that my sister-in-law was to be married. While Hemant was invited, I, again, was not. In the past, this might have shattered my confidence and made me question my worth. Instead, I recognized the emotions that such an experience triggered, took control, and reached out to my doctor to adjust my anti-depressant dosage. This experience reinforced an important lesson: self-confidence isn't about avoiding setbacks—it's about how we respond to them.

Mental health challenges can arise at any time, but they do not define our value. I've had years where I felt strong and capable, only to face unexpected events that tested my self-belief. Through it all, I've learned that seeking help is a sign of self-respect, not weakness. My doctor, who understands my journey, has reminded me that I've handled my challenges the best way I could—and that in itself is proof of resilience.

Building self-confidence starts with acknowledging your worth, even in difficult moments. It's about knowing that your voice, your feelings, and your experiences matter. You deserve to be heard—and to believe in yourself.

If you struggle with mental health, know that it doesn't diminish your worth. Speaking up and seeking support are acts of strength. I choose to be open about my journey, partly because of my grandmother, who died by suicide in 2003 when I was fifteen. She played a huge role in my life, and yet I never knew she was struggling—until it was too late. I later learned that she felt unheard and alone. That realization shaped me. From that moment on, I refused to let my voice go unheard, and committed to empowering others to do the same.

The experiences I shared here are just a short summary of the abuse I was put through by my in-laws. But I'm so glad that I didn't give up on myself and instead continued on despite the tremendous struggles. Choosing to push forward, even when it felt impossible, has been a powerful lesson in resilience and self-belief. I don't know where I would be without the unwavering support of my parents, husband, friends, and counselor, who have stood by me, encouraging me to see my worth even when I doubt myself. I have been constantly reminded that the way other people act is not my fault; it is not a reflection of me at all.

Through my journey, I've discovered that true self-confidence isn't just built by overcoming personal struggles—it's also strengthened through service to others. As I've healed, I've found purpose in supporting and uplifting those who are facing their own battles. Whether it's offering a listening ear, sharing my story to inspire hope, or simply being present for someone in need, I have realized that giving to others reinforces my strength. Helping others navigate their challenges has shown me how far I've come and has deepened my belief in my ability to make a difference. In serving, I am reminded that my experiences, though painful, have value. In lifting others up, I, too, rise—more confident, more assured, and more grateful for the journey that has shaped me.

Since moving back to New Zealand, as well as working a full-time job in the public sector, I have dedicated my spare time to volunteering for good causes and organisations close to my heart. I have served on the executive committee of the Wellington Indian Association since 2021; through this opportunity, I feel connected to my Indian culture and engage in shaping the way for Indians in Wellington, as it can be difficult to keep the Indian culture alive when living so far from India.

I have also been on the executive committee of the National Council for Women New Zealand (NCWNZ) since 2020. I discovered this organisation not long after moving back to New Zealand and felt like my participation was meant to be, considering what I had been through. This organization is an umbrella advocacy group for women's rights and fights for equality for women in all aspects of life. We organize fundraiser events for different charities and NGOs that focus on improving the lives of women. We have helped deliver petitions to parliament, put a gender lens on submissions going through government, and assisted other women-based NGOs and charities through our ties with the Minister for Women. I have found that giving back to the community and advocating for women's rights is empowering and is the cornerstone in rebuilding my self-confidence.

In 2021, I started the *Conversations with Wahine* radio show and podcast, which I co-host with other NCWNZ members. The aim of this show is to interview inspirational women and share stories that are worth talking about and listening to, bringing light to topics that are hidden under the rug. I also started the *Coconut Chats* podcast with some Indian friends in 2020. This podcast focuses on interviewing inspirational Indian people from around the world about their life journeys. Through these platforms, I have met so many amazingly inspirational people, including politicians, actors, CEOs, authors, domestic (and other) violence survivors, activists, and so many more. Wherever I can, I have used these podcasts and organisations to help women and Indians have a better and fairer life.

To date, on each platform, we've interviewed more than two hundred people, each with a completely unique and inspirational life journey. Engaging in candid conversations about people's life journeys has not only helped me heal from my past experiences of abandonment and abuse but has also reinforced my sense of self-worth. Each guest I have interviewed has shared stories of resilience, perseverance, and triumph, offering me wisdom and perspectives that have soothed old wounds. Through these interactions, I have come to realize that in giving others a platform to share their truths, I am also reinforcing my own value. The act of service—offering support, providing a space for others to be heard, and facilitating meaningful dialogue—has instilled in me a deep sense of purpose. By uplifting others, I have, in turn, strengthened my self-confidence, recognizing that my presence and my voice have the power to inspire, support, and elevate others.

I have made lifelong friends from all over the world through these podcasts, and have been invited to many prestigious events including Diwali at New Zealand Parliament, the Melbourne Cup viewing party at the Australian High Commission, morning tea with the Governor General of New Zealand at Government House, events at various embassies, and many events at the Indian High Commission of New Zealand. I was also awarded the March 2024 Vibe Lifter Award from Raglan Food Company and was a runner-up for the Mitre 10 Volunteer of the Year award in 2024. I don't do what I do for recognition and praise, but knowing that people are noticing my work gives me a sense of pride and assurance that I am doing the right thing. I cannot explain how happy it makes my heart to see that society has recognised my efforts to break down societal stigma and barriers.

I was told many times by various people not to openly talk about the bad things I went through because it would make people think I'm in the wrong, or look bad for my family, or ruin my brother's chances of getting married in the future. This is when I realized how backward Indian society still is. Although what I went through may be common in Indian culture, it does not mean it is right or should be tolerated, which is why I use my platforms to speak up about it. Rather than keep my mouth shut, I have shared my story publicly, online, and through other arenas, like I am doing here.

Women need to understand that if they are abused, they did not "deserve it" or do something to start it. An abusive situation takes two parties, and we are not responsible for how an abuser acts. We don't control anyone except ourselves, but if we are victims of abuse, we are entitled to share our story of being the victim with whomever or wherever we like, and that is what I am doing here. We are only as sick as our secrets, and openness allows our innate confidence to breathe and flourish.

Indian society also tends to not call verbal abuse "abuse." They just say, "That's how that person is," when elders behave in unacceptable ways. We respect our elders so much that we never tell them when they are wrong. This mentality needs to change. Sometimes, words, narcissism, and silence can hurt more than physical abuse and damage. Such non-physical abuse is just harder to prove because there is no physical evidence. If an abuser thinks they can abuse someone, they should also be prepared for the victim's story to come out in public. That's why I wrote this. So that no one feels alone or like their confidence is being eroded away.

I have chosen to become a much stronger person over the last few years and redirect my pain into helping women who are going through similar or even worse situations with their families or in-laws. I have seen women become shells of themselves after going through abusive situations, and I vowed to never let that happen to me. I want my voice to help the voices of others be heard so we are all treated fairly. This one decision alone has elevated my confidence, aligning with the positive impact my work has had on the community.

In some ways, I am thankful for what I went through. If my in-laws had not put me through what they did, I would not be the woman I am today and might not have gotten involved with the NCWNZ and Wellington Indian Association in the ways I have. I might've ended up being a subservient, obedient daughter-in-law who follows everything she's told, never speaks up, and tolerates being abused— or worse.

The way I see it, when one door closes (a relationship with my in-laws), another opens (using my experience to give back to society). I know I make the most of each day and my relationships with the people in my life. If others choose to close the door on people who should be in their lives, that is up to them. But I rose from the ground, and my life has only gone up from there. At the end of the day, tomorrow is not guaranteed to anyone. It is up to you how you treat people and live today.

I want you, dear reader, to see how verbal and mental abuse can affect a person's self-worth, directly affecting their confidence. The lengths I've gone through to rebuild my life, improve it, and regain my confidence shows you can do it too. I have used what I went through to help others, and that gives me a great amount of pride, because I never want anyone to go through what I did. If you are going through something similar, I want my story to help you know that you are not alone. Help is always available. If you are going through abuse of any kind, please remember, you are not alone.

"Confidence is a habit that can be developed by acting as if you already had the confidence you desire."

~ Brian Tracy

CHAPTER THIRTEEN

I Think I Can

By Leith Alayne

Self-Confidence

Self-confidence is the quiet belief in our abilities, the certainty that we can face whatever life throws our way, and the deep-seated understanding that we are worthy and capable of success. However, building self-confidence is not always straightforward, especially when it's undermined by past trauma, anxiety, or self-doubt. It is important to develop genuine self-confidence, grounded in self-awareness, resilience, and compassion.

I have experienced different types of trauma, and I know what anxiety feels like. People around me have said things to cause self-doubt. I have learned it is very important what type of people you have around you. When I was young, I had a book titled *The Little Engine That Could*. It is about believing in yourself. I had a deep feeling of belief in myself, but then people crept into my life who didn't believe in my ability, which allowed self-doubt in. Confidence was hard to find.

My confidence in myself has been a rocky ride with lots of bumps and slides—finding it and losing it at unique twists and turns.

Understanding Self-Confidence

Self-confidence is the internal acknowledgment of our capabilities and a willingness to embrace our strengths and weaknesses. In contrast to arrogance, which often tries to hide insecurity by projecting an inflated sense of self, genuine self-confidence is grounded, open to learning, and unafraid of vulnerability. It does not require comparison or validation from others.

Why is self-confidence important? When we believe in ourselves, we're more likely to pursue our goals, face challenges head-on, and recover from setbacks. Confidence bridges our abilities and potential, allowing us to step forward even in the face of doubt or fear.

I had a glimpse of confidence when I was young. There was a time when my grandmother was not kind to my mother, and I could speak up when this injustice was happening to her. My grandmother backed down because my words shocked her. Realizing that I made a difference gave me a sense of empowerment.

Identifying Sources of Low Self-Confidence

To build self-confidence, it's helpful to recognize factors that may erode it. Trauma, anxiety, and a history of criticism or failure can each play a role. Events that occur can change the way we think about ourselves. We might believe we are unloved by important people in our lives because of their actions or words, like when I walked past my grandmother's house on the way to school after she disowned us and I didn't even get a hello ninety-five percent of the time.

1. Trauma can create self-doubt, making us feel as if we're not good enough or deserving of success. Trauma's impact on self-confidence often shows up as a critical inner voice, a tendency to avoid risk, and difficulty trusting oneself. When people I loved didn't love me back, I felt worthless and incapable of doing anything successfully in any area of life. A battle occurred within me. Your value never disappears because a few people don't see it. It is always there; you are always worthy. You just have to feel it, no matter what anyone says or does.

2. Anxiety amplifies self-doubt, making small tasks seem daunting, and mistakes feel like catastrophes. It traps us in a cycle of overthinking and undermines our confidence by making us second-guess every decision. When anxiety crept in, I was too afraid to decide anything because nothing had been working out for me. I ended up frozen, unable to take steps toward anything significant. I had to take baby steps and make slow moves to find what worked and follow what made me happy. Since I struggle with acute anxiety, I knew my emotions were still active, so I used them for personal growth.

3. Past experiences with criticism or failure can also affect our self-confidence. Repeated exposure to negative feedback, especially in formative years, often leads to a tendency to downplay achievements or overemphasize weaknesses. I was told I was incapable of doing the dishes when I was young, and that belief affected my whole life without my knowledge. I didn't realize until later the impact those words had on my self-esteem. It wasn't even repeated; it was just said once from someone that loved me. Then it played on repeat in my mind, confirming the belief. It can take inner reflection to discover some of these limiting beliefs.

Recognizing these sources is the first step towards reclaiming self-confidence. By acknowledging their influence, we can separate our true potential from the limitations imposed by past experiences. Someone I loved told me I was incapable of doing anything, affecting my whole life in ways I couldn't anticipate. I believed them because they must know. It was hard to recognise because I was young. I've discovered that I am more than capable beyond what I realized. I needed to take steps—not to convince anyone— but to discover my true self and to embrace a sense of inner stability, regardless of external events.

Building a Foundation for Confidence

Self-confidence grows from a clear understanding of who we are— our values, strengths, and areas for growth. Reflecting on these aspects of ourselves can help us build a foundation of self-trust.

Identify your strengths: Write down your skills, past achievements and qualities you admire in yourself. Even small achievements can serve as reminders of your capabilities. This expertise showed me how capable I am of learning and achieving things, like coming second in a cake competition or second again in a bikini contest. Recognizing these little victories helped me rebuild my confidence. I also counted my kindness, respect, belief in others, and the encouragement offered when people are down as lovely qualities to have.

Acknowledge your growth areas: Everyone has areas to improve. Self-awareness involves recognizing where you can grow without letting these areas define you.

Identifying Your Strengths

Our strengths are the talents, skills, and qualities that define and empower us. They can vary widely, ranging from problem-solving abilities to the ability to connect with others. When we recognize and own our strengths, we create a foundation of self-belief that we can draw from in difficult situations.

Reflect on past achievements: Recall the times when you overcame challenges, succeeded in tasks, or positively affected others. Write these down to remind yourself of your resilience and abilities. These memories can serve as touchpoints, reaffirming that you can achieve your goals.

Acknowledge everyday qualities: Strengths aren't only about grand achievements; they also include the everyday qualities that make you who you are. Are you a good listener, a dedicated worker, or a creative thinker? Don't overlook these qualities. Often, they are the quiet superpowers that bring value to our lives and those around us.

Consider feedback: Sometimes others see strengths in us we might overlook. Think about compliments or positive feedback you've received from colleagues, friends or family. This helps you recognize abilities you may have taken for granted.

Knowing Your Values and Passions

Self-confidence involves not only understanding what we're good at but also knowing what matters to us. Our values and passions serve as guiding principles and motivate us toward goals that align with who we truly are.

Identify your core values. Values are the principles that matter most in life. Do you value honesty, creativity, compassion, or learning? Understanding your values helps you make decisions that align with your true self, giving you the confidence to pursue paths that resonate with your identity.

Explore your passions: Passion often points us toward our unique contributions. Reflect on activities or topics that excite you or draw your interest. When we pursue our passions, we naturally feel more confident and energized, as these pursuits often bring out the best in us. I value kindness and love, and I respect pursuing things like writing, swimming, gardening, and helping others.

Embracing Growth Areas

True self-confidence involves acknowledging that we all have areas for growth. Rather than viewing these as limitations, seeing them as growth areas allows us to adopt a mindset of continuous improvement, where every experience is an opportunity to learn.

Be open to constructive feedback: Receiving feedback can feel intimidating, but it offers valuable insights. Seek feedback from people you trust and view it as a guide rather than a judgment. Recognizing areas where we can improve strengthens self-confidence because it allows us to approach life with humility and resilience.

Building Self-Trust Through Authenticity

When we are clear about who we are, we can show up authentically in our lives. Authenticity is a powerful element of confidence because it allows us to feel aligned with our inner truth. When I was honest with myself about how people were treating me, it gave me a sense of freedom to make new decisions that took me to places I had never been before.

Align actions with values: When we make choices that align with our values, we build trust in ourselves. Living authentically empowers us to approach life confidently, knowing we're honoring our true selves rather than trying to fit someone else's expectations.

By continuously understanding, embracing, and working with who we are, we lay the foundation for genuine self-confidence. This confidence isn't based on being flawless but on knowing that, whatever life brings, we are capable and worthy, just as we are.

Set Realistic Goals

Building self-confidence comes from small, achievable goals that allow you to grow at a steady pace. Each accomplishment, no matter how small, strengthens your belief in your abilities and keeps your momentum going. I have had goals from just to making it through a day to moving to a new place and starting from scratch with nothing. Looking at how far I have come helps me set new goals.

Begin with manageable goals that are easy to achieve. Break down larger goals into smaller steps, and celebrate each success. As small wins add up, they keep you motivated. For example, writing a chapter wasn't as easy as I thought it would be, but I did it one word and one paragraph at a time.

Set "stretch goals" just outside your comfort zone, challenging enough to foster growth without overwhelming you. Focus on effort over outcome, as each attempt builds confidence and expands your comfort zone.

My stretch goal has been to complete this chapter. Another was helping a client reprogram her mindset because she focused on the negative. She needed reminding that words and thoughts are powerful and what she tells herself is important. I focused on helping her become aware of what comes out of her mouth.

Make goals specific and trackable to keep yourself focused. Instead of "I want to improve at public speaking," try "I will give a short presentation by month's end." Tracking progress reinforces confidence and shows your growth.

Check in regularly to see if your goals align with your current priorities. Be open to adjusting goals as needed, and raise the bar as you grow to keep building confidence without slipping back into old comfort zones.

Setting realistic goals is about creating a sustainable path to self-confidence, where each step reinforces your belief in yourself. With every small success, slight stretch and lesson learned along the way, you build confidence that is grounded, resilient and ready to support your growth.

Develop a Growth Mindset

A growth mindset—the belief that skills can improve through effort and learning—builds lasting self-confidence. With this perspective, setbacks become learning opportunities, and confidence grows from the process of improvement, not perfection. As a support worker, I help people daily with their mindset and lives. It was uncomfortable walking into the homes of people I didn't know, but the more I did it, the more comfortable it became.

Treat setbacks as feedback rather than failures. Ask, "What can I learn?" This mindset builds confidence and self-assurance, knowing each attempt brings growth. When setbacks happened in my life, I understood that I wasn't aligned with the outcome I desired. Although it can be sad and I did nothing wrong, I didn't dwell on what was—I kept thinking and feeling my way forward.

With a growth mindset, confidence becomes rooted in the journey of learning, adaptability, and ongoing progress.

Cultivate Patience and Self-Compassion

Growth doesn't happen overnight, and it's essential to be patient and kind to yourself along the way. Practicing self-compassion allows you to focus on gradual improvement rather than perfection, fostering a steady and sustainable confidence.

There are days when self-acceptance is all I have to give. When my energy level is down and I feel like I can't face the day, I tell myself, "It's ok. There is always tomorrow." I became my own biggest supporter.

Be patient with yourself. Progress is often incremental, so remember that both confidence and growth take time. Embracing a long-term view allows you to appreciate the journey, making it easier to stay committed without getting discouraged by temporary setbacks. Treat yourself with the same kindness you would offer a friend. Self-compassion means recognizing that you're human, with strengths and areas for growth, and that each step forward is valuable. This mindset nurtures a sense of confidence rooted in acceptance, not perfection.

No matter what is happening in my life, I face people choosing not to talk to me, work cancellations, expectations, or deadlines. I take everything in stride and understand that other people's choices have nothing to do with me. Knowing I'm worthy of kindness and communication has been a necessary acknowledgment for myself.

Positive Self-Talk with "I Am" Statements

The way we speak to ourselves directly shapes our beliefs and self-image. By shifting our self-talk into affirming "I Am" statements, we reinforce our identity in ways that align with self-worth, confidence and capability. For instance, instead of saying, "I'm not sure if I can handle this," try, "I Am capable of learning and growing through this." When we say, "I Am confident," we start embodying belief in ourselves as a confident person. This technique can feel powerful because it affirms who we are, not just what we do. "I Am" are the two most powerful words you have in your vocabulary. You can use them positively and negatively. "I Am" gives power to whatever comes after it.

I personally don't have just I am statements. I also use I feel, I do, I love, I speak, I see and I know. Here are some examples of mine:

I am safe.
I feel one with all and I do so with love and kindness.
I love to be at peace.
I speak with confidence.
I see the truth, and I know with all my heart.

Visualization with "I Am" Identity Anchoring

Visualization can become even more effective when you incorporate "I AM" affirmations. Imagine your most confident self, picturing how you would look, feel and act. Anchor this visualization with statements like, "I AM confident," or "I AM empowered." This process reinforces self-confidence at an identity level, helping you feel naturally inclined to take confident actions. I do this before going to sleep. I wake up ready to work toward my goals with empowered feelings and self-confidence to tackle each task.

Daily "I Am" Journaling Practice

Reflecting on affirmations in a journal reinforces self-belief over time. Begin each day by writing down a few "I Am" affirmations, such as "I Am worthy of success," "I Am learning to trust myself" or "I Am resilient in the face of challenges." This ritual helps reinforce these beliefs daily, shifting your mindset and nurturing a confident self-image.

When I first started doing this, I came from a dark, sad, and down place. After my affirmations, I felt a change in my emotions. The strength from within grew daily as well as new little accomplishments.

Celebrate Small Wins

Celebrating small wins is essential to building lasting self-confidence. Instead of waiting for big achievements, recognizing each step forward reinforces our belief in our abilities, keeps us motivated, and builds a sense of progress. I celebrate the small wins by treating myself to getting my nails done or taking myself out to dinner.

Celebrating small wins nurtures a compassionate relationship with ourselves, helping us appreciate progress rather than criticize what's left to do. This self-acceptance strengthens confidence by valuing each stage of our journey. Making celebration a daily habit—like keeping a journal or reflecting on small wins—creates a positive feedback loop that reinforces self-confidence as a natural part of life. Celebrating each small victory keeps us motivated, reinforces our growth, and reminds us that each step forward is worth acknowledging—creating a self-confidence rooted in resilience and self-compassion.

Embrace Vulnerability

Embracing vulnerability is a powerful way to deepen self-confidence. By allowing ourselves to be open, honest, and imperfect, we build resilience and trust in our ability to face life's challenges authentically. Vulnerability helps us move beyond a need for perfection and gives us the courage to show up as we are, reinforcing a self-confidence rooted in self-acceptance and growth.

I feel most vulnerable when I am with myself in the moment. In the past, I was around people who judged me so harshly that I changed myself to be accepted. Now I don't care what people think and I will always be myself.

True self-confidence doesn't require perfection; it comes from accepting ourselves as we are. By embracing vulnerability, we permit ourselves to be human, acknowledging that imperfections and mistakes are natural and part of the journey. Each time we accept our flaws, we reinforce self-compassion, strengthening our self-confidence. Instead of hiding our insecurities, we can recognize that being open about them is an act of courage—one that shows our strength rather than weakness.

When we allow ourselves to be vulnerable, we open the door to deeper, more authentic relationships. Being honest about our fears, challenges, or areas where we need help creates connections based on trust and understanding. These genuine connections support our self-confidence by reminding us that we are not alone in our experiences. Knowing we're supported and understood by others gives us the courage to be our authentic selves and strengthens our belief in our worth.

Embracing vulnerability means we're willing to take risks and face potential failure, knowing that we'll grow regardless of the outcome. Trying new things and putting ourselves out there doesn't always guarantee success, but it always guarantees growth. This shift from a fear of failure to a growth mindset helps us become more resilient, reinforcing self-confidence as we learn to value progress over perfection. Each time we take a risk, we prove to ourselves that we can handle both success and setbacks.

Building Confidence in Social Situations

For many people, social situations can trigger self-doubt. Developing self-confidence in these contexts involves focusing less on what others think and more on staying true to yourself.

Prepare, but be flexible. While it's helpful to prepare for challenging social interactions, be open to change. Don't script your responses; instead, focus on being present and engaging in active listening. I do this by promising myself to be considerate and truthful in my interactions, with open ears and an open heart.

Use body language to your advantage: stand tall, maintain eye contact and use open gestures. Positive body language can help you feel more in control and project confidence, even when you feel nervous. This became a habit after entering enough homes I didn't really want to go into. I practiced taking a deep breath, telling myself I can do this, reminding myself to be myself and saying to myself, "Leith, you've got this."

Moving Forward: Confidence as a Practice

Self-confidence is not something we achieve once and have forever. It's a practice we must return to daily. With each effort—whether it's reframing negative self-talk, celebrating a small win, or embracing vulnerability—we strengthen our confidence. I maintained consistency with my confidence muscle by developing the daily habit of using all the tools I've shared with you.

Remember, self-confidence is less about the absence of fear and more about the decision to act despite it. With time, patience, and practice, you can cultivate a sense of self that is strong, resilient, and ready to face the world on your terms.

"Confidence means showing up even when you feel uncertain."

~ Unknown

CHAPTER FOURTEEN

--------∽oↃ⌒Ↄo∼--------

Unseen, Unshaken: My Journey to Unstoppable Confidence

By Kelly Graver

There's a silence that comes with pain when no one can hear it or see it. For most of my life, I lived in that silence, navigating a world that seemed oblivious to the battles I fought daily. Living with an invisible disability is often like walking against a fierce wind. Every step forward requires an effort that goes unseen, but the strain is constant. It's not just the disability itself that wears you down; it's the feeling that the world carries on as if everything's fine while you're struggling to survive.

It wasn't always easy for me to talk about these things. I grew up in a home that was very private. I was taught to carry my burdens quietly. Speaking about my struggles felt like breaking an unspoken rule, as if bringing them into the light would make them too real. So, I learned to keep my battles tucked away, out of sight and out of mind. At least, that's how it seemed to the outside world, except for the select few who were close to me.

Before my world drastically changed, I was a competitive swimmer training at an Olympic level, swimming up to ten miles a day. My life revolved around the water, exercise and fitness, a place where I felt powerful and whole. The mental, emotional, and physical discipline required was intense, but I thrived on it. That all shifted when I faced three serious injuries, each one compounding the last, and multiple instances of malpractice that left me wheelchair-bound. The losses hit hard, stripping me not only of physical ability but also of a part of my identity. I didn't just lose my strength. I lost my confidence, and rebuilding it became the greatest challenge of all.

With each setback, my self-confidence took a profound hit, and I began questioning my worth and my future. I eventually received a diagnosis: a genetic connective tissue disorder called Ehlers-Danlos syndrome. This disorder affects every tissue and joint in the body. Ehlers-Danlos compromises the very structure holding my body together. My connective tissue, the essential "glue" that supports my skin, muscles, tendons, and organs, is fragile and unstable. Even simple movements can feel excruciating, like my joints are slipping or tearing with every step. Pain is a constant companion, and injuries that most people recover from can linger, worsening over time. It's a disorder that doesn't just affect one part of me; it affects every layer of my being, amplifying every physical struggle and making daily life feel like an endurance test.

Years later, I was repeatedly exposed to toxic black mold, a hidden threat that nearly cost me my life. I lost everything I owned—my home, all of my belongings, my money, my savings—I became homeless, and my health and immune system took a drastic hit. I battled lung damage, severe environmental and chemical sensitivity, and eventually, cancer.

Early Stages & Struggle

Adjusting to a life so different from the one I'd known was nothing short of devastating. When you're stripped of the things that once defined you, it's as though pieces of your identity slip away, one by one. I went from feeling like an unshakeable force in the world to someone who was barely able to get out of bed, let alone get through the day. It wasn't just the physical limitations that challenged me; it was the sudden absence of purpose and direction. I had spent years building my life around a dream only to watch it dissolve before my eyes.

The people around me tried to be supportive in their own ways, but I often felt their words fell short, like they couldn't quite grasp the depth of what I was going through. Friends would say, "You're strong," or "Just be positive," but they couldn't relate and didn't see the despair lurking beneath my brave face. I slowly started to become more and more isolated, struggling to articulate what I was feeling to anyone. How could they understand the weight of dreams lost to a body that no longer felt like my own? Living this way not only drained my life-force but eroded my confidence in a world that failed to see me.

As the weeks turned into months and months turned into years, I questioned everything about myself. Self-doubt crept in slowly, like a fog rolling in over the water until it became all I could see. Thoughts like, "What if this is my life now?" and "Who am I without my abilities?" played on repeat, each one chipping away at the confidence I once took for granted. I wanted to believe there was a way forward, but I couldn't imagine a future where I could feel capable again. My days felt empty, my sense of purpose dimmed, and my faith in myself dwindled.

The most painful part was that those around me couldn't see the silent battles I fought. Outwardly, I looked like the picture of health, the kind of body that could have graced the cover of a magazine. But inside, it was a different story, one of pain and limitation. People would say, "You don't look sick," or "You just need to try harder," but they only saw the surface, the mask I wore to survive each day. They didn't see the endless nights I laid awake, muscles and joints aching in ways I couldn't describe, or the constant calculations I made in my mind just to get through simple tasks.

And then there were those who didn't just misunderstand; they refused to believe me. They told me it was all in my head, that I was exaggerating or that I simply needed to "push through it." Friends, even family members, questioned the reality of my pain. Some people accused me of making it up, as if the toll it was taking on my life wasn't proof enough. The disbelief and doubt stung more than any physical pain because it left me feeling terrified. Who could I trust? Where could I turn for safety and healing? We heal in connection and community, in the presence of those who see and believe us. But instead, I felt abandoned, invisible and entirely alone.

Being doubted, gaslighted, and dismissed cut deeply, isolating me in a way I hadn't expected. I found myself shrinking as the world around me seemed to deny my very real and very painful experiences. My body was struggling, my spirit was breaking, and yet, to everyone else, I looked fine. That dissonance between how I felt and how I was perceived was perhaps the hardest part of all.

Being stuck in an ongoing crisis, where you rarely get reprieve and the people around you don't recognize or validate what's happening, is one of the worst things I think a human can experience.

I longed for someone to witness my pain and acknowledge what I was going through; each comment telling me to "Try harder," or "Just get over it," made me question myself. I had once been so strong, so capable. How could this be happening to me?

Turning Point: Choosing Confidence

There comes a point in every struggle when you're forced to make a choice: keep letting it consume you or decide to fight back in a way that feels true to who you are. For me, that moment wasn't a grand revelation but a quiet realization, a whisper beneath the weight of my doubts. After years of feeling trapped in an endless cycle of pain, rejection, and invisibility, I knew that something had to change. Not the circumstances themselves, but how I responded to them.

With the help and guidance of a few remarkable therapists, wise mentors, compassionate coaches and spiritual teachers, I saw a new way forward. They helped me untangle the fear that had taken root inside me, showing me how to move toward the very things that scared me the most rather than retreating behind the maladaptive coping strategies I had relied on to feel safe. It wasn't easy—growth never is—but in facing my fears head-on, I discovered a strength I didn't know I had. This journey didn't aim at becoming fearless; it was about learning to live with fear as a companion, stepping forward despite it and trusting in my ability to navigate the unknown.

One day, after a particularly grueling moment, I sat in the stillness and asked myself a hard question: what would it look like to start fully believing in myself again? The answer wasn't immediately clear, but it sparked a shift within me. I realized that confidence wouldn't come from a miracle cure, a change in circumstances or the validation I'd once craved from others. It would have to come from within, a decision I would need to make daily. I had to choose confidence, grit and faith even if it felt like a foreign concept in the face of my reality.

I began reclaiming small pieces of myself. I set tiny goals, ones that to others might seem insignificant but to me felt like monumental victories. Some of the goals were getting out of bed on days when my body felt like lead, reaching out to people even when isolation seemed easier and simply looking in the mirror and acknowledging my resilience rather than my weaknesses. Each act, however small, felt like a statement: "I'm still here, and I'm still fighting."

At first, I was met with resistance, not only from my doubts, but from the world around me. But I didn't owe anyone an explanation. Confidence wasn't for them to understand or validate. It was a gift I was giving back to myself. There was power in that choice. By choosing to trust in myself with one hundred percent of my heart and soul, I slowly began to redefine my sense of self-worth.

A pivotal part of my journey was learning to embrace the word "disability." For so long, it had felt like a label drenched in negativity, something society equated with weakness, shame or inadequacy. But as I faced my fears and reclaimed my sense of self, I began to see the word differently. Disability didn't make me less; it made me different. In that difference, I found unique strengths and perspectives that I could honor with pride. Learning to claim the word with dignity and self-respect became a powerful act of defiance against societal narratives and an essential piece of building my confidence. It was no longer a term to shrink from, but a badge of honor, a testament to the battles I had fought and the resilience I had built.

I realized that confidence isn't the absence of pain or struggle; it's the decision to stand up, time and time again, even when you're not sure of the outcome. Confidence became my anchor, my way of reclaiming who I was, separate from my limitations. Each day, as I chose confidence anew, I found pieces of myself I thought I'd lost. A quiet endurance, strength of will, and an unwavering sense of self.

Building Unstoppable Confidence

Choosing confidence was just the first step. I knew that if I wanted it to last, I'd need to strengthen it like a muscle, nurturing it through the storms and reinforcing it every day. Confidence isn't something you find once and hold onto; it's something you build piece by piece, moment by moment. And each choice I made, no matter how small, helped me move from a fragile belief in myself to something unstoppable.

One of the first things I did was establish daily rituals that kept me grounded, small practices that reminded me of my tenacity and worth, even on days when doubt crept in. Every morning, I began with a few simple mantras:

- I am brilliant, worthy and enough just as I am.

- I am deeply proud to be me.

- I honor the trauma and experiences that I've had, while also opening up more deeply when I feel ready.

- I am safe in my body. My body is not working against me, but fighting with me and for me. We are a sacred team.

- I set and hold healthy boundaries and advocate for myself with confidence and clarity.

- I live in and accept the present moment without judgment.

- The world needs me to share my value and gifts and I say yes.

- My soul has chosen this journey, and I choose it too. I'm here, ready and deeply committed to my growth.

At first, the words felt hollow, more like wishful thinking than truth. But over time, they sank in, slowly reshaping my inner dialogue. Saying those words each day was like laying a brick in a wall that protected me from self-doubt. Gradually, I began to embody them, not just in my thoughts but in the way I moved through the world. During my mantras and meditations, I envisioned these truths taking root within me as if my cells were reprogramming themselves to believe in my worth and strength. This was the true power of manifestation—not in wishing for a different life, but in aligning my mind, body, and spirit with the life I was ready to create.

I also made a commitment to celebrate small victories. Living with my disabilities, my accomplishments might seem trivial to others. Things like walking a few extra steps, making it through the day with less pain or finding a way to laugh despite the challenges. But I came to see that every small step was part of a larger journey. By recognizing these wins, I built confidence not on grand achievements but on a foundation of persistence, determination and the courage to keep moving forward.

Building unstoppable confidence also meant learning to face my fears head-on. I no longer waited for the world to validate my worth. Instead, I began trusting my inner voice. Each time I acted on that voice, whether by setting a boundary, standing up for myself, or choosing to rest when I needed it, I gave myself permission to believe in my strength. Little by little, my confidence became like a lighthouse, something steady I could rely on, even when life's waves threatened to pull me under.

Alongside this growing inner strength, I realized the importance of levity amid the heaviness. Joy and humor became my favorite medicines. They didn't erase the pain or change my circumstances, but they lightened the burden, reminding me of the parts of myself that hardship could never reach. Joy and laughter became a way to reconnect with who I was at my core.

Finding moments of joy amid discomfort taught me something profound about confidence: it's not about pretending to be invincible. It's about realizing that we can bend without breaking. Humor helped me reclaim a sense of agency, reminding me I could shape my experience, even when I couldn't change the outcome. Laughter didn't erase the struggle, but it gave me the courage to face it with an open heart. Joy showed me that I could find completeness, even amid the chaos, by choosing to embrace life exactly as it was.

Confidence is the understanding that we can carry both joy and sorrow, light and darkness, and still move forward. Each smile, each laugh and each moment of joy reminded me that my spirit remained open to possibility.

To anyone who feels like confidence is out of reach, I say this: let joy and humor be your guides. Don't wait for the perfect moment to invite them into your life. Welcome them into the imperfection, the mess, and the struggle.

Redefining My Dreams

When I first began this journey, my dreams seemed like fragile things, remnants of a life I could no longer return to. The aspirations I had, a future defined by physical strength and pushing limits, felt painfully out of reach. But as I worked to rebuild my confidence and find new ways of valuing myself, I realized that maybe my dreams didn't have to disappear; maybe they just needed to change shape.

Redefining my dreams meant finding new ways to make an impact, ways that didn't rely on physical ability but drew on my resilience, my confidence, my compassion, my endless curiosity, my creative expression, and my deeper understanding of what it means to overcome. I started asking myself different questions. What could I create that would be meaningful not only to me but to others? How could I use my experiences to make a difference, to inspire or empower others who might be facing their own struggles? These questions led me to see that my journey had equipped me with unique insights and strengths that could fuel new dreams. Ones that didn't require me to be physically strong but emotionally strong, wise, and open-hearted.

One of the first dreams I redefined was to be a voice for others who felt invisible, like I had once felt. I realized my story could be a source of strength for someone else, that maybe, by sharing my experiences, I could help others feel seen and validated. Writing became a way for me to shape this dream. A path that allowed me to reach people who might be in their own storms, feeling as if no one could understand. Each word I wrote became a pillar in the foundation of a new purpose—a dream rooted not in what I had lost, but in what I could still give.

Redefining my dreams also meant learning to embrace creativity in ways I hadn't before. I started exploring new passions that weren't bound by my physical limitations. I found fulfillment in creative expression, in discovering new ways to bring beauty and meaning into the world. I began turning my pain into art. Through teaching, coaching, mentoring, writing poetry, music, comedy, storytelling, and connecting with others on a deeper level, I realized my dreams could be expansive, reaching beyond the limits I had once known.

Redefining my dreams became an act of self-love, a way of honoring the person I was becoming, rather than mourning the person I once was, which simultaneously nurtured my self-confidence.

In the end, these new dreams brought me a sense of fulfillment I hadn't expected. They gave me a reason to keep moving forward, a purpose that extended beyond my struggles. My dreams had transformed, shaped by resilience and a deep commitment to living a life that felt true to who I was. Someone who had faced unthinkable challenges and emerged with a heart open to new possibilities.

The Hands That Carried Me Home

When the ground beneath us crumbles, it is the unwavering love of our friends, family and chosen family that becomes the bridge back to ourselves. A powerful reminder that none of us carry the weight of this life alone.

When life shattered in ways I couldn't have imagined, I quickly learned who my real friends were. These beautiful souls didn't just stand beside me—they entered the wreckage with me. They weren't fair-weather friends; they were my spiritual warriors, my ride-or-die companions. We didn't just walk through the fire together—we roasted marshmallows in it. My friends and family have been the foundation of my healing and the wind beneath wings.

These were the people who stayed, not out of obligation, but out of love. They held my hand through the darkest nights, when words weren't enough, but their presence spoke volumes. They laughed with me when life's absurdities became too much to bear and cried with me when the weight of it all was too heavy for one heart. They laid beside me in hospital beds, their quiet presence turning sterile rooms into spaces of connection and hope. These were the people who didn't need me to be strong, who didn't ask for explanations, who simply stayed—fully present, fully loving, fully believing in me when I couldn't believe in myself.

It was through their steady love and belief that I saw my worth again and was able to trust that I was strong, capable, confident and deserving of the life I envisioned. They didn't just support me; they dreamed with me, painting visions of a future I couldn't yet see. They problem-solved alongside me, turning obstacles into challenges we could face together, even if the solution was simply to sit still and breathe. Their love didn't just offer comfort; it offered transformation. Each laugh we shared, each tear they wiped away, each whispered "You're not alone" became a thread in the tapestry of my healing, stitching together the pieces of a heart I thought had shattered beyond repair.

Healing doesn't happen in isolation. It happens when someone is willing to meet us in our darkest places and walk alongside us. My friends and family weren't perfect—no one is—but that's what made their love so extraordinary. It wasn't about flawless support; it was about showing up, consistently and wholeheartedly. One of my friends once joked, "If we can't fix it, let's at least eat snacks and laugh at how bad it is." And so, we did. We ate, we laughed and we found our way through the mess together. Their humor and unwavering commitment were medicine for my soul. Their love reminded me of the profound truth that Ram Dass spoke: "We are all just walking each other home."

To these very special people, I owe my deepest gratitude. Your presence was a gift I could never repay. Each of you, in your unique way, brought something extraordinary into my life—a kindness, a wisdom, a love that only you could give. You are the reason I kept going, the reason I found my way back to myself. To say you gave me wings would be an understatement! You helped me rediscover my own. Through your love, I rebuilt not just my confidence but my faith in what it means to be seen, held and cherished. You reminded me I was lovable exactly as I am and that together we could rise, no matter how far I had fallen. Your love was a healing balm, your faith in me a lifeline. You showed me that true friendship is a rare and sacred bond, built on the simple but profound act of showing up, time and time again. And for that, I thank you with all my heart.

To you, the reader, I want to share something that took me far too long to learn: ask for help. Asking for support is not weakness; it's wisdom. It's a courageous act of self-love to let others in, to allow them to be part of your journey. Find your sacred support system. Find the people who believe in you, who will walk with you through the fire. Allow their belief in you to guide you back to your own heart. Let them hold your hand as you find your way back to yourself and they will remind you, as my friends reminded me, that none of us walk this path alone.

Lessons in Confidence

As I look back on this journey, I see now that confidence was never about appearances, accomplishments or even strength in the traditional sense. True confidence is something much deeper; it's a quiet knowing that lives in the soul, a choice we make to keep believing in ourselves, even when everything around us falls away. It's the courage to stand in our truth, even when that truth is met with resistance, judgment, criticism, silence, or disbelief.

Confidence isn't given; it's created, woven out of each choice we make to show up for ourselves.

There were days I thought I would never feel whole again, when the weight of loss and the sting of abandonment, pain, isolation and invisibility threatened to pull me under. But each time I faced those moments, something within me refused to give up. Living with an invisible disability has taught me that real strength often goes unseen. It's the strength that doesn't rely on acknowledgement from others because it knows that the most important battles are the ones we fight within.

What I have come to know, through the chaos and the quiet revelations of life, is the enduring truth of my spirit. I have always carried within me an unapologetic free spirit, a bold and uninhibited nature that refuses to be contained. I have a spirit that will not bow to convention and craves freedom as much as air. My enduring spirit has been my lifeline, a quiet rebellion against the forces that sought to shrink me. Even in my darkest hours, my spirit flickered, a force both wild and steady, urging me to remember who I am.

Rediscovering my confidence was not a recovery, it was an unearthing. It was pulling up the roots of who I was and examining them with reverence. Confidence is a force that doesn't shout—it hums, it is not something you project—it is something you inhabit. It doesn't seek approval; it resonates. It is the quiet power of living in harmony with the truth of your being, unyielding to the world's attempts to define you. When you find it, it shifts everything. When you find it, you find freedom.

I have dedicated my life to making art out of my suffering by weaving something transcendent from what might have broken me.

And in doing so, I've uncovered a joy so rich it feels almost defiant. I now teach others to alchemize their pain into something luminous, to embrace the raw materials of their lives and craft them into masterpieces. My life is far from perfect, but it is mine, and that makes it exquisite. It is real, vibrant, authentic and cherished, just like the spirit that's carried me through. And for that, I love my life deeply and without reservation.

To anyone reading this who feels unseen, unheard or unworthy, know that your worth is not defined by the judgement of others. You carry within you the same spark, the same inner strength that has guided me through my darkest hours. Confidence isn't something you have to prove—it's something you come to know deep in your bones.

I hope that these words remind you that you are already enough, that your spirit holds an infinite well of strength, fortitude, and beauty. So, as you walk your path, remember this: confidence is not just a promise—it is a declaration, a roaring truth that you are worthy, capable, and unstoppable. May you summon the courage to dive deep into your heart, to stand tall in your truth, and to find peace in the uncertainty, knowing that every step—no matter how small— brings you closer to the life you are meant to live. Trust fiercely in your ability to rise, again and again, no matter how many times you have to begin. You are not defined by what has happened to you, but by the fire in your spirit and your refusal to give up.

Now, take this moment—this breath—and choose yourself. Choose to believe in your strength, your beauty and your boundless potential. When the weight of the world feels heavy, let this be your rallying cry: I am here, I am unstoppable and I will thrive.

"The way to develop self-confidence is to do the thing you fear and get a record of successful experiences behind you."

~ William Jennings Bryan

CHAPTER FIFTEEN

Building Self-Confidence

By John R. Spender

E veryone wants to be a bit more confident, regardless of where they are in life and I'm no different. Knowing that you can trust your judgement, abilities and qualities is a completely different feeling than the uncomfortable place of not believing in yourself. It's natural to feel unsure when you are first learning a new skillset, but it's having the humility to develop a beginner's mindset to ask questions, research, course-correct, and learn through action that supports a lasting, grounded confidence.

Building self-confidence helped me go after what I wanted to do as opposed to staying with the safer option. Don't get me wrong— there's nothing bad about choosing the safer option and being in your comfort zone as long as you're moving towards something meaningful in life. However, when you have confidence in yourself, you can experience what life truly has to offer. I'll let you know right off the bat that my comfort zone held me back from quite a lot of fulfillment because I didn't trust that I could get the job done.

Things changed as I became more and more confident. I started taking risks and went after things that meant something to me. I'm not saying that I won every single time, because I didn't. There were quite a lot of failures too, but my entire journey of self-confidence helped me grow as a person and allowed me to become comfortable in my own skin.

What Does Self-Confidence Really Mean?

I first started creating a connection with my spirit to truly get to know myself and build confidence. I had an epiphany on January 26, 2010, after snorting lines of coke in the toilets with a buddy. While washing my nose at the sink, I glimpsed myself in the mirror and I didn't like what I saw. I despised my reflection and myself for using some stupid powder to boost myself up. I was angry, betrayed and I wanted to smash the mirror.

I decided then and there that I was going to make some serious changes, but I lacked a structured approach. Instead, I let divine guidance lead me to a book about living a fulfilling life online. It was called *What I Wished I had Learned at School* by Jamie McIntyre. It resonated with me, as I had a successful landscaping business and traveled all over the world, but didn't feel completely fulfilled. Something was missing, but I didn't know what it was.

Ten years earlier, I had a fifteen-person staff and large council contracts around Sydney, including one contract at an Olympic Games site in Darling Harbour. On the outside, it looked like I was going places and filled with confidence, but inside, I didn't know who I really was. I had suppressed aspects of my past, including significant emotional, physical, and sexual abuse. I had built a brick wall around these memories. The problem was, these unloved parts started to rot, and I found myself self-medicating with cocaine. The habit became so strong that I completely destroyed my business and nervous system. It took around five years to rebuild my confidence until I felt I could start again, this time with a focus on lifestyle.

In this particular case, it was easy to confuse confidence, self-confidence, and arrogance. At face value, they all appear to be the same, but they're drastically different. Understanding the distinction between them is key to gaining clarity.

While arrogance is somewhat different, both confidence and self-confidence are tied to each other. Self-confidence is an attitude or belief you have about your skills and abilities. Having self-confidence means that you:

- Accept and trust that you have control in life.

- Know what your strengths and areas of improvement are.

- Set realistic expectations and goals.

- Are capable of handling criticism.

Apart from this, I like to separate self-confidence into two categories: high and low. If your perception of yourself aligns with the points I've mentioned above, you probably have a certain level of self-confidence. However, if you feel inferior to others, that things in life just happen to you, or you constantly doubt yourself, chances are you have low self-confidence. That was me when I first joined Toastmasters. I felt like an imposter and was terrified someone would uncover the truth of how terrified I was at any moment.

It's taken me quite a few years to learn how to receive constructive feedback. I remember when I first went to Toastmasters, a leadership and speaking organization, to practice my public speaking skills. By then, I already had a year of consistent practical experience under my belt and I had done well in several training programs. This experience included delivering weekly presentations at Mission Australia for three months, delivering a keynote talk at a coaching boot camp for life coaches and practicing in my lounge room with a couple of friends who also wanted to get paid to present from stage. Additionally, I had completed several intensive speaker training programs, like T Harv Ecker's Train the Trainer, Platform Skills with Christopher Howard, and Making the Stage with T Harv.

At my first Toastmasters meeting, I delivered my Icebreaker speech. I phoned the club, signed up on the call and booked my first speech. The members were shocked by my decision to deliver my first speech without attending a meeting beforehand. My mentor used to always say, "Start with confidence, and the competence will follow."

A friend joined me and we signed up for two clubs. I delivered a speech at every weekly meeting I attended. I participated in their contests and consistently delivered talks at other clubs throughout Sydney.

I eventually moved to Bali, running NLP trainings in Singapore for a US company based in Ubud. After completing the contract in 2013, I hired a mentor who helped me transition my coaching practice to an online platform before online coaching became popular or the term "digital nomad" existed. At the time, my confidence was only surface-level and not yet built on a solid foundation of inner knowing.

During this phase of my spiritual development, I cared too much about what other people thought of me. I felt like I was in a paradigm of thriving but never arrived or was completely satisfied with myself. I was avoiding my feelings and showing vulnerability, which is the birthplace of authentic grounded confidence, where I can feel unsure or uncomfortable but still show up with a sense of self-belief.

Self-confidence comes from belief, while confidence comes from experience, exposure, and past victories. These factors are interconnected. The way I see it is that you first need to believe in your abilities—meaning you have self-confidence—and when you move forward with that belief you either succeed or learn from it. That, over time, gives you grounded confidence.

Arrogance, on the other hand, is more about having an inflated sense of self-importance and feeling superior to others. One of the many things I've picked up on is that while both self-confidence and confidence are positive traits, arrogance is not. This is quite a mainstream idea, but from my perspective, many people don't fully grasp what it means.

I found myself wanting to exaggerate my abilities, achievements, and experience, all coming from a place of insecurity. The exaggeration itself made me feel superior to others. Naturally, all of us want to share our achievements so we can get some applause, and this honest need for appreciation can turn into the fear of not being enough. Wanting a pat on the back now and then is okay, as long as you can keep that need in check. What I found helpful to understand here is that external appreciation leads to developing a need for constant validation. Having developed a need for constant validation, I never felt like I was winning until people clapped for me.

The biggest problem with this was that this need fueled my arrogance. I needed a *"superior"* status to feel validated and to feel enough. I didn't keep this need in check, and it led to an arrogant, dismissive, condescending, and uninterested attitude. I couldn't accept that no one wins all the time. When I was arrogant and lost, I wasn't open to feedback and suggestions from others because I no longer felt superior and that was a scary place to be. This held me back from improving my skills and abilities, which in turn kept me from being of service to others. Over time, the belief I had in my skills and abilities faded away, meaning I had no self-confidence.

This is quite a conundrum to be stuck in, and I found that out the hard way. I was afraid to ask for support when I needed it the most. I masked my need for help, pretending everything was under control. From my experience, the easiest way to steer clear of this is to have faith in what you can do, but don't think that you're the only one who can do it. It's helpful to open up to learning and improving!

Fear of Criticism or Failure: A Hurdle or a Tool—You Decide!

By now you have an understanding that self-confidence is belief in one's skills and abilities. However, when it comes to building self-confidence, it's also about understanding that fear of criticism or failure can be both a hurdle and a tool.

Fear can keep you from believing in yourself, especially if you have low self-confidence to begin with—meaning you don't fully trust your capabilities. I've come to believe that a vulnerable state of mind allows fear to take root and become stronger. Fear like this leads to the development of a negative self-image, which is how you see yourself. If you have a negative self-image you'll think you're unworthy or incapable.

You've heard it before; fear lies and I'm not going to tell you anything different. It does lie. I am going to shed some light on how the lie plays out in life. When we put effort towards learning something or working on something, we expect a certain type of result. Some of us even have a mental picture of what that result should be. More often than not, we believe success is achieving that result and not achieving it as a failure. We don't want to fail, so we become obsessed with how we can get the result we want. With that obsession comes the fear of failure or criticism. This fear is what held me back from trying things, and it probably has the same effect on you.

When we fail to achieve a goal, our beliefs about our skills and abilities receive neither external nor internal validation. In addition, the criticism we receive, both from ourselves and others, further points out our believed inadequacy. It feels like you spent six months training for the 100-meter dash, and collapsed after the first twenty-five meters. It's important to understand that winning validation, whether external or internal, is not the goal. In fact, seeking validation develops arrogance and a weak self-image.

The goal should be to improve. When you look at it this way, you'll see that validation, although somewhat essential, is not of enough value to be concerned with and failure can be used to gain valuable insights for improvement.

Consider this: If someone is afraid to try because of the fear of failure, the beliefs they have about themselves never get tested. The confidence and self-confidence they have exists only in a fabricated, self-comforting environment. When push comes to shove, and it will, that person will likely fail, especially if they have unresolved, emotionally significant events. This is what happened to me with my first landscaping business. The pressure of managing staff and contracts stretched me beyond what I could handle. It became too much, and I resorted to other means to deal with my internal implosion.

Comparison and Developing Self-Confidence

Not many people think of this, but when we look at others, we often see things they have that we don't. When we have low self-confidence or a negative self-image, we never trust our own capabilities. This lack of trust in one's self goes on to reinforce our perception that someone else is better, which leads us to see only what we lack.

While it's important to compare ourselves to others, going about it the wrong way can be detrimental. You might already be familiar with the concept that "comparison is the thief of joy," but when it comes to developing self-confidence, it can have both positive and negative outcomes. Healthy comparison is necessary, but to make sure it's not harmful, you need to understand how it negatively affects self-confidence. Some of the ways include:

1. Fostering Self-Doubt

   Self-doubt, as the name suggests, occurs when someone doesn't believe in themselves. Such doubt can stem from comparison, especially when we see others without context. For example, we can look at someone who achieved what you were trying to in six months, without taking into account the resources they had at their disposal.

   We end up using their achievement as a metric for our own success. Comparison without context can make us feel that we're not capable of achieving the same result, which, in turn, leads to self-doubt and deters the self-confidence we had.

2. Promoting Unrealistic Standards

   Another negative effect of comparison is that it only promotes highlights, not absolute reality. Take, for example, a fitness influencer who lost twenty pounds in five weeks and is now selling a course that helps others achieve the same thing. The problem here is that many people start seeing the influencer as a metric or goal to compare themselves to. However, not a lot of these people understand that the course might not be the only thing the influencer used to achieve their physique. A person who buys the course might expect the same result and when they fail to achieve those results, they think the problem lies with them. This again initiates the chain of self-doubt and deters self-confidence.

3. Developing a Fixed Mindset

Both the reasons I've mentioned above, and others like them, lead to the development of a fixed mindset. Constant negative comparisons can make you feel like you'll never be as good as others. Not many people understand the magnitude of this problem. The worst part? Not many people, my former self included, know they're facing it.

What this mindset does is develop a false precedent that says if you've failed to meet your goals five times, you will not succeed the sixth, seventh, or however many other times you try. This mindset keeps you from trying and diminishes the belief and trust you have in your abilities.

I've gone through many of these experiences when I was building self-confidence, and one thing that stuck out to me was the fact that where comparison is harmful, it can also be beneficial.

When we compare ourselves to others, we are either consciously or subconsciously setting a benchmark. Comparison is beneficial to us if we look at what others have achieved and how far we are from those achievements. After this, we can analyze the achievement itself to determine areas where we fell short and improve based on those insights.

In addition, healthy comparison can also serve as a source of inspiration and knowledge. When we compare ourselves to someone who has excelled in an area we wish to, we can gain insight from them. For example, if you want to improve public speaking, figuring out what experts do and comparing what you're doing can help bridge the gap.

What comparison does for you depends on how you use it. Here's how I used comparison to help me develop self-confidence: instead of comparing myself to others, I compared my current self to my previous self at regular intervals. You can do it every month or after a few months. The goal is to be honest in your evaluation and see how far you've come. This will reinforce your belief in your skills and in your ability to learn, adapt and grow.

I always admired what others achieved, but I never let their achievements undermine my own potential. If someone achieved a goal in four weeks and I only achieved 50% of the same goal in four weeks, that didn't affect me negatively. It just told myself I needed four more weeks and used comparison to figure out what I needed to do to achieve my goal faster.

The aim of positive comparison is to observe others and learn from them. You can do this by talking with the person you're comparing yourself to. Most people are reluctant to do this, but trust me, if you're comparing yourself to the right people—those who are on a journey of betterment themselves—you'll find that they're more than happy to help.

Above all else, comparison has taught me that everyone is running their own race. You are not up against someone else. Your goal is not to be better than someone else, but to be better than you were the day before.

Practical Tips for Building Self-Confidence

These are tips that I've followed for quite a long time in my life and they're worth a shot to build and increase self-confidence.

Identify Strengths and Weaknesses

When you're aiming to develop self-confidence, the first thing that you need to determine is what your capabilities and areas for improvement are. Identifying your strengths and weaknesses will help you determine where you need to direct your efforts. However, it's important to have some sort of balance between utilizing your strengths to achieve what you can and improving areas where you lack.

Set Realistic Goals

When you've figured out what you're capable of, you need to set goals based on those insights. Remember that self-confidence means believing in your abilities, and your results will either strengthen or weaken that belief. So, it's essential that you set goals that are challenging but still within your reach, as this will allow you to test your capabilities while learning and improving from difficulties.

Take Care of Yourself

Going after a goal day in and day out, is something everyone, including me, is guilty of. But, what you need to understand is that this approach will bleed you dry, and sooner rather than later, the motivation is going to run out and you'll find yourself off track. It's better to practice self-care by eating healthy, sleeping well, and having mental clarity. This will help you be more consistent and that's the winning ingredient.

Eliminate Negative Self-Talk

All of us criticize ourselves when we fail or don't get the desired result. While healthy criticism is important, you must make sure that such criticism does not translate into negative self-talk, constantly undermining yourself and your abilities. It can lead to a loss of motivation and hope. To eliminate this, try positive affirmation techniques and you'll see the difference yourself.

Remember that self-confidence is the belief you have in your skills and abilities. It's not something you're born with, but something you develop over time. Confidence grows through the experiences where that belief is tested. Each time you face a challenge and push through it, you strengthen your sense of self-assurance. But don't expect to feel confident all the time, because the path to true confidence isn't linear—it's filled with ups and downs. And that's okay. The setbacks are just as valuable as the wins because they teach you how to adapt, persevere, and bounce back stronger.

Along the way, both fear and comparison are inevitable. Fear can be a major roadblock or a powerful motivator, depending on how you approach it. When fear arises, don't shy away from it. Instead, see it as an opportunity to reflect on what you truly value and what you're capable of. Fear only has power over you when you allow it to control your actions. Use fear to your advantage by acknowledging it and then taking deliberate steps to move forward, even if it's with small, careful actions.

Similarly, comparison can either hold you back or propel you forward. When you compare yourself to others, it's easy to feel inadequate or discouraged. Instead of letting those feelings of envy or insecurity take root, use them as tools for growth. Let the success of others inspire you, not defeat you. Their achievements can show you what's possible and what's achievable. Instead of focusing on how you measure up to others, focus on how you can learn from them and use their example to challenge yourself to improve.

In the end, remember that your only aim is to be better than you were yesterday. This isn't about perfection; it's about progress. Every small step forward, every lesson learned, and every challenge faced is a victory in its own right. Focus on your journey, knowing that self-confidence will grow when you consistently put in the effort to evolve and push past your limits. Trust the process, be kind to yourself, and keep working toward becoming the best version of yourself. Your future self will thank you for the confidence you show today.

"The real glow-up is when you stop waiting for validation and start believing in yourself."

~ Unknown

AUTHOR BIOGRAPHIES
James Greenshields

CHAPTER ONE

James is a mystical man with a huge heart and a vision to match. He is a husband of over 20 years, and honoured father of two amazing women, with a flavour for the deep esoteric dive. His experience with post-traumatic stress, after serving in Iraq, set him on a path to learn all he could about healing the causal issues. The success of his healing journey is evident, and he describes himself as a man who lives with post-traumatic growth!

In the 14 years post military, James co-founded and been the Lead Facilitator for Leadership and Men's Wellbeing at Emergent Leaders Foundation. There's not much this man hasn't touched from experiences with First Nation people around the globe, running youth rites of passage for ten years, overlaid on practical understanding of leadership in environments as complex and diverse as the battlefield, boardrooms, and professional sports have enabled him to create a new paradigm of leadership - Harmonic Leadership.

With a firm belief that every issue on the planet can be solved at a community level within a global context, James has just spent the last two years assisting communities around Australia become self-sufficient. A major part of this work has been shifting their consciousness and laying a leadership platform from which to lead.

Facebook: https://www.facebook.com/james.greenshields1/
Instagram: https://www.instagram.com/jamesgreenshields/
Linked In: https://www.linkedin.com/in/james-greenshields-41705a5/
YouTube: @JamesGreenshields29
Website: www.emergentleaders.org
Email: james@emergentleadersfoundation.org

Linda Orr-Easo

CHAPTER TWO

Linda Orr-Easo is a licensed Spiritual Practitioner, NLP Coach, Trainer, and Energy Worker whose personal journey, including two burnouts, has opened her up to the Truth that within our very essence, this is where we find our True Self. All our beliefs, thoughts, feelings, words, and actions are simply choices that we make. When Linda rediscovered this, she felt such a tremendous sense of relief that she no longer needed to pretend, to be someone that other people or situations expected her to be. It was then that she began living what she calls her authentic life.

As Linda reconnected within and became more aligned with her Soul, she quickly began to see her whole life flow so beautifully. It was as if a door had been opened to the infinite possibilities that she had somehow hoped were there but until then she had never really experienced this in her daily life to this extent.

Given the impact of the above on Linda's life, she knew that her mission was to help as many people as possible open to the Truth and the incredible power within to create the lives we desire.

Linda runs workshops, offers small group and 1:1 coaching, and is now an author with her first book on wealth—*The 6-step Spiritual Path*—due out in 2025.

www.beatha.ch
contact@beatha.ch.

Emily Moon

CHAPTER THREE

Emily is a New Earth visionary, intuitive, channel, and higher self-embodiment guide. She weaves intuitive guidance, channeled messages, light language, and sound energy, among other modalities, into her offerings to help support others on their spiritual journey and empower a deepening connection with their higher self

She is incredibly passionate about helping others cultivate a deeper relationship with their higher self where life can be experienced with more trust, ease, playfulness, and ultimately more Freedom! Empowering others to move beyond "outgrown" versions of oneself to step forward into the "new" version of self with confidence is also one of her great joys! From her own journey, she knows what's possible and holds this vision for All.

Emily loves to travel, immerse herself in peaceful nature, and experience life as our playground!

She offers 1:1 sessions as well as in-person/online events, workshops, and retreats. Her e-newsletter offers support tools, inspirational messages, and upcoming events. If you would like to receive, please subscribe online www.HigherDimensionsWithin.com/newsletter.

Email: Emily@HigherDimensionsWithin.com
Website: www.HigherDimensionsWithin.com
1:1 Sessions: www.HigherDimensionsWithin.com/sessions
IG/FB: @HigherDimensionsWithin

Emeryelle Moore

CHAPTER FOUR

Emeryelle loves to be an example of what it can look like to honor your experience and learn how to enhance it through purification and restoration of the mind, body and soul. In 2012, she received a diagnosis of stage 4 endometriosis after the first of two life saving surgeries before finding her answer to reversing illness through holistic health.

Over the last two decades Emeryelle has delved into the fields of business, art, creativity, health, wealth and higher consciousness following her passions and desires. In 2021, she began answering the call to teach and now leads private cohorts sharing what she has learned through holistic restoration from severe endometriosis, asthma and unlocking the innate healing systems of the human body.

Through her journey of revealing how our bodies heal she began to deeply unlock ancient wisdoms, spiritual gifts and multi-dimensional awareness. Emeryelle also leads private cohorts in the field of mediumship, electromagnetic restoration, consciousness expansion, ancient healing and wisdom.

Emeryelle is on her way to deepening her practice and level of support through obtaining a tri-doctorate in Holistic Health, Botanical Herbalism and Functional Medicine. She dotes on the importance of self care, a well-loved and tended to family life and being one example of how we can achieve harmony and symbiosis in our own home which is where she believes the biggest impact truly begins.

You can find her on social media at https://www.facebook.com/EarthAngelEmeryelle or email her directly at emeryellemf@gmail.com

John Kelly

CHAPTER FIVE

Personal and Executive Transformative Supercoach, John F Kelly isn't your typical coach. While he boasts an impressive 30+ year career in senior sales, marketing, and leadership positions, his true passion lies in empowering individuals and organisations to reach their full potential. This passion fuelled John's journey beyond the corporate world.

He invested heavily in personal development, focusing on coaching, business strategy, culture development and transformative performance methodologies. His work with renowned coach Michael Neill unlocked for John a profound truth: that within each of us lies a beautiful design brimming with infinite potential waiting to be unleashed.

John's understanding of human potential, spirituality and well-being, makes him a thought-provoking and inspiring transformative supercoach and speaker. His mission is to share this understanding. John wants to help people fall back in love with life and rediscover the breathtaking possibilities within each of us. Forget limitations, embrace fearlessness, and live a life filled with love—that's the transformation he believes is on offer to all of us.

https://www.linkedin.com/in/johnfkellyfxl/
https://www.facebook.com/JohnKellyConnects/
www.johnkellyconnects.com

Kristen Dolan

CHAPTER SIX

Kristen Dolan has been a Network Marketing professional for almost 15 years. She absolutely loves the industry and all the ways it provides each individual with what they need, whether it's products, supplements, a community, an income, leadership skills, personal development, she knows people will always receive what they need most. Kristen deeply values her role in guiding and coaching people on their journey of self-discovery.

She believes we all have goals and dreams in life that our everyday jobs are limited in helping us achieve. While no one grows up envisioning themselves selling skincare, protein shakes, or supplements, we also are rarely asked what kind of person we want to be when we grow up. That is exactly what Network Marketing did for Kristen—it gave her the tools to become the best version of herself.

Being a mom to her twin daughters and spending her days asking people what kind of person they want to be—while helping them create the tools and resources to make it happen—has been more rewarding than she ever could have imagined. It all started with being offered an opportunity to dream again—something she had forgotten how to do for herself.

Joanne Mengwasser

CHAPTER SEVEN

Joanne is a certified life coach with over seven years of experience, dedicated to helping individuals navigate personal and professional challenges with confidence. She holds a college degree in textiles, and her passion for quilting has been a vibrant part of her life for over 40 years.

As an avid quilter, Joanne has been actively involved in multiple quilting groups and has shared her expertise by teaching quilting to others.

Beyond her creative pursuits, Joanne has a rich 16-year career in e-learning, where she has contributed significantly to advancing educational technologies. Her compassionate nature was also reflected in her role as a caregiver for her parents prior to their passing, demonstrating her commitment to family and community.

Joanne's diverse background and empathetic approach enable her to connect deeply with her clients, guiding them towards personal growth and fulfillment. Her ability to weave together her life experiences enriches the support she offers, making a positive impact on all those she works with.

Facebook link:
https://www.facebook.com/profile.php?id=100029409378295
Website link: https://www.loveyourlifecoaching.co/

Heather Price

CHAPTER EIGHT

Heather Price is a shamanic healing practitioner/trainer, coach/mentor, author, ceremonial woman and visionary. She is in service to assist those who walk with her to live, love and lead in spirited ways, and to create a path of vibrant health and wellbeing. Heather aspires to develop conscious communities and working environments, inspiring confidence and self-awareness through sacred practices.

Heather teaches *The 8 Ways: Shamanic Guidelines for Walking Consciously and Confidently in the World*. She sees the mandala, drum, and labyrinth as instruments for presenting her teachings and bridges between the worlds within, without, above, and below. She imagines herself as a guide, linking people between these worlds.

Heather reminds those who walk with her that when you come to know your strengths as well as your challenges, you are able to walk and lead more freely and confidently in personal and professional spaces.

She is passionate about writing and has co-authored a number of collaborative publications and written two e-books to support personal development and vision planning.

Website: https://www.shamanicpathandpractice.com
Email: info@heatherprice.net
Facebook: https://www.facebook.com/shamanicpathandpractice
Twitter: https://twitter.com/#shamanicpath

Oksana Aya

CHAPTER NINE

Oksana was born and raised in Ukraine until she was 15. Ever since moving to the US, she has gone through countless transformative life experiences that led her to become the person she is now—and still becoming.

As a nurse practitioner specializing in oncology, Oksana combines medical expertise with a deep commitment to holistic healing. A Reiki Master, skilled in hypnosis and sound healing, she brings a unique blend of science and spirituality to her work, empowering others on their own journeys of transformation.

Beyond her professional accomplishments, Oksana is most proud of being a mother to Sophia. Balancing her career, healing work, and motherhood, she inspires others with her unwavering faith and belief in the power of authenticity and clarity.

Oksana's passion for healing and humanity continues to drive her every action. She envisions the human body as a radio, perfectly designed to receive the divine guidance and messages of the universe, much like a radio captures a song from the airwaves. However, if the radio is not properly tuned, the message comes through as static—distorted or incomplete.

Her mission is to help individuals fine-tune their inner frequencies, aligning their minds, bodies, and spirits so they can clearly receive and harmonize with the melody of divine wisdom and purpose.

Email: OksanaAya@yahoo.com
FB: Oksana Aya

Julian Mann

CHAPTER TEN

Julian Mann is a dedicated Three Principles facilitator and author, with over fourteen years of experience in working in mental health services. He is dedicated to supporting others on their journeys towards uncovering their innate wellbeing. Julian believes in a human-to-human approach having found that removing the therapist/patient dynamic an essential component of empowering his clients to find their own answers.

His calm approach to helping others comes without any judgement because it is rooted in his own experience, having struggled with and overcome depression. He uses his insights to gently guide others to look deep within themselves where their own mental health is waiting to be uncovered.

In addition to his work as a facilitator, Julian has been sought after to give talks and presentations around the world.

Julian believes that happiness comes not from living a life free of challenges, because, if you are a human being, that is impossible. Rather, happiness comes from our ability to understand and navigate those challenges when they arise.

Through his compassionate approach, extensive experience, and personal journey of overcoming adversity, Julian Mann stands as a beacon of hope for those who are struggling and cannot see a way through. His work embodies the essence of empathy, knowledge, and unwavering support, making him an invaluable resource for those in need of a helping hand.

Kim Frazer

CHAPTER ELEVEN

Kim is no stranger to the world of inspiration. She began her success in leadership as a youth. She went on to be very successful in coaching a team in cosmetic sales and is a light to all who know and love her.

Kim's laughter is contagious, and she inspires others to be better. Through her life's journey she learned that bounce back ability and a mindset shift were what drove her, whether she was up or down. Keeping her eye on the prize and the desired end result brought a spark to her spirit.

She loves helping others evolve in their highest, best selves. Kim has traveled through many ups and downs, as we all do. Each time she came back stronger and more grounded, loving, authentic and aware.

Her greatest spiritual awakening came when her father crossed over to heaven after a pancreatic cancer diagnosis. Kim's family fought for his life—he was the pillar—and great love remains. This intense grief brought about that lesson that none of us are getting out of here alive, make your time count.

A gift has been growing a best friendship with her mom along the way. Kim is family-focused and driven by her dreams to make a difference for the masses—and she's doing it!!

Be sure to follow her on social media.

Rise to your grounded, authentic, loving awareness, because it is knocking. Answer the call.

Harita Gandhi-Kashyap

CHAPTER TWELVE

Harita Gandhi-Kashyap is a third generation New Zealand born Indian on her mums side, and first generation on her dad's. She is an accountant by profession. She grew up performing Bharata Natyam (a form of classical Indian dance) and Bollywood dancing. These were very important to keeping her culture alive, living so far from India and growing up in a part of Wellington that didn't have many Indian people.

Growing up, Harita never thought she would become so heavily involved in volunteer work and women's rights advocacy. However, events throughout her life have led her to this work in recent years and she thoroughly enjoys it, knowing she is doing all she can to help women and Indian people have better, fairer, and happier lives.

Harita has been the treasurer of the Wellington branch of National Council of Women NZ since 2020 and the publication secretary of Wellington Indian Association since 2021. She is a co-host of two podcasts: Coconut Chats, which focuses on interviewing inspirational people of Indian descent from all over the world, and Conversations with Wahine, which focuses on interviewing inspirational New Zealand women.

She lives in Wellington with her husband and their two cats, Mewtwo and Raikou, whom they adopted from a shelter in 2024.

Leith Alayne

CHAPTER THIRTEEN

Leith – A Heart Full of Kindness and Strength

Leith, 51, originally from Brisbane and now residing in Hervey Bay, embodies compassion, resilience, and a profound dedication to others. As a support worker, her natural ability to connect and care for those in need shines. Leith's unwavering patience and understanding have allowed her to succeed where others could not, supporting even the most challenging clients with grace and empathy—once supporting a client for six months when others could not assist beyond a single day.

A devoted mother to three adult children, Leith has overcome significant personal challenges, including a marriage breakup and the end of a 15-year abusive relationship. Through these experiences, she has grown into a strong, independent woman who balances her innate selflessness with a newfound commitment to caring for herself.

Leith finds joy in swimming, gardening, and nurturing her plants. She often dreams of traveling and embraces a love for learning. Her values are rooted in kindness and spreading love, believing that "everything you touch with love is touched by love."

Leith's uplifting spirit, encouraging nature, and protective instincts bring warmth and positivity to everyone around her. She is a true testament to the power of compassion and the beauty of a life lived with love at its core.

Kelly Graver

CHAPTER FOURTEEN

What happens when a Behavioral Scientist, a Wellness Counselor, and a Relationship Expert walk into a bar… of wisdom? You get Kelly Graver—a self-proclaimed "Psychology Geek" with over 15 years of experience in the personal development space.

Kelly is the founder, head coach, and Chief Mentor at Connected Hearts Coaching. She draws from her extensive and diverse education in psychological methodologies, including Health Psychology, Sexual Psychology, Attachment Theory, and Positive Psychology. In addition, she is certified in a range of therapeutic modalities such as Internal Family Systems (also known as "Parts Work"), Relational Trauma Therapy, Organic Intelligence, Mindfulness Meditation, and Stress Management.

Kelly's philosophy is grounded in the fusion of Western psychological principles and Eastern practices. A deep believer in the healing power of nature and the art of spiritual alchemy, she guides individuals and couples toward profound transformation by fostering self-awareness, accountability, and intentionality in body, mind, and spirit. In doing so, she believes we not only uplift our own lives but create a ripple effect of healing and connection in the world around us.

As a writer, public speaker, and truth seeker, Kelly infuses deep compassion with a fearless sense of humor. Her work is an invitation to embrace life's complexities—turning chaos, curiosity, and cosmic insight into meaningful art, resonant words, and transformative wisdom. Her goal is simple: to help people rediscover their essential power and transform their lives into extraordinary adventures.

John R. Spender

CHAPTER FIFTEEN

John R. Spender is a 39-time international best-selling co-author who didn't learn how to read and write at a basic level until he was ten years old. He has since traveled to more than 75 countries and territories and started numerous businesses, leading him to create the best-selling book series *A Journey of Riches*. He is also an award-winning international speaker and filmmaker.

John worked as an international NLP trainer and coached thousands of people from various backgrounds through many challenges. From borderline homeless individuals to wealthy people, he has helped many connect with their truth to create a life on their terms.

His search for answers to living a fulfilling life has taken him to work with Native American Indians in the Hills of San Diego, visit the forests of Madagascar, swim with humpback whales in Tonga, explore the Okavango Delta of Botswana, and climb the Great Wall of China. John has traveled from Chile to Slovakia, Hungary to the Solomon Islands, the mountains of Italy, and the streets of Mexico.

Everywhere his journey has taken him, John has discovered a hunger among people to find a new way to live, with a yearning for freedom of expression. It was during this journey that his belief that everyone has a book in them was born.

He is now a writing coach, having worked with over 400 authors from 50 countries for the *A Journey of Riches* series (http://ajourneyofriches.com/). His publishing house, Motion Media International, has published 45 non-fiction titles to date.

John also wrote and produced the documentary movie *Adversity*, which will be released later in 2025 and stars Jack Canfield, Rev. Michael Bernard Beckwith, Dr. John Demartini, and many more. You can bet there will be a best-selling book to follow.

"Confidence is not about being perfect; it's about accepting your imperfections and still feeling worthy."

~ Unknown

AFTERWORD

I hope you enjoyed the heartfelt stories, wisdom, and vulnerability shared. Storytelling is the oldest form of communication, and I hope you feel inspired to take a step toward living a fulfilling life. Feel free to contact any of the authors in this book or the other books in this series.

The proceeds from this book will be used for social giving at Jewel Children's Home in Northeast Bali.

Other books in the series are...

Unlock Your Hidden Potential, Book Thirty-Nine
https://www.amazon.com/dp/B0DXVKT6KH

Follow Your Soul's Calling, Book Thirty-Eight
https://www.amazon.com/dp/B0DQJYLBHY

The Power of Self-Discovery, Book Thirty-Seven
https://www.amazon.com/dp/B0D4K35JFP

Elevating Your Life: A Journey of Riches, Book Thirty-Six
https://www.amazon.com/dp/B0CZWRJ94Y

Living the Paradigm of Kindness: A Journey of Riches, Book Thirty-Five
https://www.amazon.com/dp/B0CSXF1FBV

Creating Resilience: A Journey of Riches, Book Thirty-Four
https://www.amazon.com/dp/B0CNVRDY38

Discover Your Purpose: A Journey of Riches, Book Thirty-Three
https://www.amazon.com/dp/B0CFDLWTCB

Live Your Passion: A Journey of Riches, Book Thirty-Two
https://www.amazon.com/Live-Your-Passion-Stories-Fulfilling-ebook/dp/B0C5QXMNRQ

Master Your Mindset: A Journey of Riches, Book Thirty-One
https://mybook.to/MasterYourMindset

Transform Your Wounds into Wisdom: A Journey of Riches, Book Thirty
https://www.amazon.com/dp/ B0BKTJ377N

Motivate Your Life: A Journey of Riches, Book Twenty-Nine
https://www.amazon.com/dp/B0BCXMF11P

Awaken to Your Inner Truth: A Journey of Riches, Book Twenty-Eight
https://www.amazon.com/dp/B09YLYMQ4H?geniuslink=true

The Power of Inspiration: A Journey of Riches, Book Twenty-Seven
http://mybook.to/ThePowerofInspiration

Messages from The Heart: A Journey of Riches, Book Twenty-Six
http://mybook.to/MessagesOfHeart

Abundant Living: A Journey of Riches, Book Twenty-Five
https://www.amazon.com/dp/B0963N6B2C

The Way of the Leader: A Journey of Riches, Book Twenty-Four
https://www.amazon.com/dp/1925919285

The Attitude of Gratitude: A Journey of Riches, Book Twenty-Three
https://www.amazon.com/dp/1925919269

Facing Your Fears: *A Journey of Riches,* Book Twenty-Two
https://www.amazon.com/dp/1925919218

Returning to Love: *A Journey of Riches,* Book Twenty-One
https://www.amazon.com/dp/B08C54M2RB

Develop Inner Strength: *A Journey of Riches,* Book Twenty
https://www.amazon.com/dp/1925919153

Building your Dreams: A Journey of Riches, Book Nineteen
https://www.amazon.com/dp/B081KZCN5R

Liberate your Struggles: A Journey of Riches, Book Eighteen
https://www.amazon.com/dp/1925919099

In Search of Happiness: A Journey of Riches, Book Seventeen
https://www.amazon.com/dp/B07R8HMP3K

Tapping into Courage: A Journey of Riches, Book Sixteen
https://www.amazon.com/dp/B07NDCY1KY

The Power Healing: A Journey of Riches, Book Fifteen
https://www.amazon.com/dp/B07LGRJQ2S

The Way of the Entrepreneur: A Journey of Riches, Book Fourteen
https://www.amazon.com/dp/B07KNHYR8V

Discovering Love and Gratitude: A Journey of Riches, Book
Thirteen
https://www.amazon.com/dp/B07H23Q6D1

Transformational Change: A Journey of Riches, Book Twelve
https://www.amazon.com/dp/B07FYHMQRS

Afterword

Finding Inspiration: A Journey of Riches, Book Eleven
https://www.amazon.com/dp/B07F1LS1ZW

Building your Life from Rock Bottom: A Journey of Riches, Book Ten
https://www.amazon.com/dp/B07CZK155Z

Transformation Calling: A Journey of Riches, Book Nine
https://www.amazon.com/dp/B07BWQY9FB

Letting Go and Embracing the New: A Journey of Riches, Book Eight
https://www.amazon.com/dp/B079ZKT2C2

Making Empowering Choices: A Journey of Riches, Book Seven
https://www.amazon.com/Making-Empowering-Choices-Journey-Riches-ebook/dp/B078JXMK5V

The Benefit of Challenge: A Journey of Riches, Book Six
https://www.amazon.com/dp/B0778S2VBD

Personal Changes: A Journey of Riches, Book Five
https://www.amazon.com/dp/B075WCQM4N

Dealing with Changes in Life: A Journey of Riches, Book Four
https://www.amazon.com/dp/B0716RDKK7

Making Changes: A Journey of Riches, Book Three
https://www.amazon.com/dp/B01MYWNI5A

The Gift in Challenge: A Journey of Riches, Book Two
https://www.amazon.com/dp/B01GBEML4G

From Darkness into the Light: A Journey of Riches, Book One
https://www.amazon.com/dp/B018QMPHJW

Thank you to all the authors who have shared aspects of their lives, hoping to inspire others to live a larger version of themselves.

I want to share a beautiful quote from Jim Rohn, "You can't complain and feel grateful at the same time." At any given moment, we can either feel like a victim of life or be connected to and grateful for it. I hope this book helps you feel grateful and inspires you to pursue your dreams.

For more information about contributing to the series, visit http://ajourneyofriches.com/. If you enjoyed reading this book, we would appreciate your review on Amazon to help share our message with even more readers.

www.ingramcontent.com/pod-product-compliance
Lightning Source LLC
Chambersburg PA
CBHW051944090426
42741CB00008B/1259